COMPUTER PROGRAMMING
BEGINNER'S GUIDE

THIS BOOK INCLUDES:

*LEARN SQL AND COMPUTER
PROGRAMMING JAVASCRIPT*

ADAM HARRIS

Table of Contents

Learn sql:

Computer programming Javascript:

LEARN SQL:

Introduction

What is SQL?

Before you can begin experimenting with SQL, you must have access to a database system. There are various online SQL editors you can use to evaluate or test SQL statements I have provided as examples in this book. However, you need a full-fledged database management system in order to execute SQL statements.

Basic Terms

What is Relational Database?

A relational database is a type of database categorized into tables with each table relating to another within the database. It allows data to be divided into smaller, logical, and manageable units for better performance and easier maintenance. To relate one table to another, you need to create a common field or key in a relational database system.

Definition Data

Data is a fact that relates to a particular object under consideration. For instance, your name, weight, height, weights are unique to you. You can also consider a file, image, or picture as data.

Definition Database

A database is a systematical collection of data. Through a database, you can manipulate and manage data easily. For instance, your electricity supply has a database to manage your billing, address, and other relevant information. Another example is your famous Facebook account; it contains information relating to your friends, messages, member activities, pictures, etc.

Definition Database Management System

DBMS is a collection of programs enables users to access database, report, manipulate, and represent data. Furthermore, it allows users to control access to the database. DBMS is not a new concept and was first implemented in the 1960s.

Types of Database Management System

- *Hierarchical DBMS* – this uses a "parent-child" relationship in storing data. People hardly use them nowadays. However, it has the structure of a tree with nodes representing records. An example of this type of DBMS is the registry used in Windows XP
- *Network DBMS* – This DBMS allows many-to-many relationship. For beginners, this is a complicated database structure. An example is the RDM server.

- *Relational DBMS* – This kind of DBMS defines a database relationship in terms of tables. Unlike the network DBMS, relational DBMS doesn't allow many-to-many relationship. Example of relational DBMS includes a Microsoft SQL Server database, Oracle, and MySQL.
- Object-Oriented Relation DBMS – *This allows the storage of new data types. Data are stored in the form of objects*

Setting Your SQL Work Environment

Peradventure you don't have any database management system in your computer, you can opt for various free open source database management system. You can decide to opt for the famous MySQL, which can be downloaded for both Windows and Linux operating systems.

Furthermore, you can install SQL Server Express, which is a free version of Microsoft SQL Server. Otherwise, you can decide to install XAMPP or WampServer. The WampServer is a Windows web development environment that allows you to create a MySQL database, PHP, and Apache2.

SQL Syntax

SQL Statements – These statements are simple and straightforward like your normal English language. However, they have specific syntax. Don't form your own meaning when you see some of the common English words you are conversant within this chapter.

An SQL statement comprises of a series of keywords, identifiers, etc. and ends with a semicolon (;). The following is an example of a SQL statement:

SELECT stu_name, DoB, age FROM studentFile Where age > 20;

The statement may look clumsy but for better readability, you can rewrite it in this format.

SELECT stu_name, DoB, age

FROM StudentFile

WHERE age > 20;

The purpose of the semicolon is to submit the statement to the database server or terminates the SQL statement.

Case Sensitivity in SQL

Keywords in SQL are not case sensitive like the previous languages discussed in this book. For instance, the keyword SELECT is the same as the select. However, depending on the operating system, the table names and database can be case-sensitive. Generally, Linux and UNIX platforms are case-sensitive, unlike Windows platforms that are not case-sensitive.

The example below retrieves records from the studentFile table

SELECT stu_name, DoB, age FROM studentFile;
select stu_name, DoB, age from studentFile;

The first one capitalizes the keywords whereas the second isn't capitalized. It is better to write SQL keywords in uppercase in order to differentiate it from other text.

SQL Comments

Similar to other programming languages, SQL comments are ignored and provide quick explanations concerning the SQL statements. You can either use a single-line or multi-line comments when writing comments in SQL. The two examples below will distinguish both comment writing formats.

```
--Select all the students
SELECT *FROM studentFile;
```

To write a multi-line comment, you use the /* with the statements followed by the */.

```
/* Select all the students

 whose age is greater than 20*/

SELECT *FROM studentFile

WHERE age > 20;
```

Database Creation

Before you can work with data, the first thing to do is to create a database. I am assuming you have installed the SQL Server or have MySQL in your system. Furthermore, ensure to allow every necessary privilege needed.

There are two ways of creating a database

- Using the simple SQL query
- *Using MySQL*

Simple SQL Query

The syntax for creating a database in SQL is

```
CREATE DATABASE databaseName;
```

```
CREATE DATABASE studentFile;
```

Note: You can also use CREATE SCHEMA rather than using CREATE DATABASE to create a database. Additionally, creating a database doesn't make it available for use. To select the database, you have to select the database using the USE statement. For instance, the USE studentFile; command will set the StudentFile database as the target database.

MySQL Database Creation

I will use a command line tool to create a database in MySQL.

Step 1: Invoking the MySQL command-line tool

To do this, you have to log into your MySQL server. You have to log in as a root user and enter your password when asked. If everything goes right, you will be able to issue SQL statements.

Step 2: Creating the database

> To create the database "studentFile", you have to execute the following command.

```
mysql> CREATE DATABASE studentFile;
```

If the database was successful, you will see – Query OK, 1 row affected (0.03 sec). However, if the database already exists, an error message will display. Therefore, to avoid such situation, you can include an optional clause – IF NOT EXISTS. To apply it to the example, it will be written as:

```
mysql> CREATE DATABASE IF NOT EXISTS
studentFile;
```

Step 3: Selecting the Database

If the database already exists and you use the IF NOT EXISTS statement, to select this new database as the default database, you have to select it.

```
mysql > USE studentFile;
```

Tip – in order to see all the list of existing databases when using MySQL server, you can use the "SHOW DATABASES" keyword to execute it.

Creating Tables in SQL

So far, I am convinced you now know how to create a database. It is time to upgrade your knowledge in SQL by creating a table inside our database. The table will hold the data in the database. The purpose of the table is to organize your data or information into columns and rows.

The syntax for table creation

CREATE TABLE tableName (

Column1_name data_type constraints,

Column2_name data_type constraints,

Column3_name data_type constraints,
    );

For better understanding, I will create a table in our studentFile database using the MySQL command-line tool. The code below simplifies that.

```
-- Syntax for MySQL Database

CREATE TABLE studentRecord (

    id   INT   NOT   NULL   PRIMARY   KEY
AUTO_INCREMENT,

  Studname VARCHAR(50) NOT NULL,

  DoB DATE,

  phoneNum VARCHAR(15) NOT NULL UNIQUE

-- Syntax for SQL Server Database

CREATE TABLE studentRecord (

  id INT NOT NULL PRIMARY KEY IDENTITY(1,1),

  Studname VARCHAR(50) NOT NULL,

  DoB DATE,

  phoneNum VARCHAR(15) NOT NULL UNIQUE

);
```

The code above creates a table named studentRecord with five columns id, Studname,

DoB, and phoneNum. If you observe, a data type declaration succeeds each column name.

In a database table, every column must have a name followed by a data type. The developer decides on the particular to use, depending on the information to store in each column. From the example above, some statement looks "foreign" and requires explanations. Later, I will talk about the various data types but to familiarize yourself with them, they include:

- Exact numeric
- Approximate numeric
- Date and time
- Character strings
- Unicode character strings
- Binary strings
- Other data types

Besides the data type, there are constraints used in the code. Constraints are rules defined concerning the values permitted in columns. The following constraints were mentioned.

- The PRIMARY KEY constrains, which marks the corresponding field as the primary key for the table
- The NOT NULL constraints, which make sure fields cannot accept an unacceptable value

- The AUTO_INCREMENT attribute, which automatically assigns a value to a field left unspecified. It increases the previous value by 1 and only available for numerical fields.
- *The UNIQUE constraint ensures every single row contains a unique value in the table*

In a similar fashion, you can use the IF NOT EXIST statement we used when creating a database to overwrite an existing table. This is important as it avoids any already existing table. Alternatively, if you want to display available tables, you can use the SHOW TABLES statement.

```
CREATE TABLE IF NOT EXISTS studentRecords (

    id    INT    NOT    NULL    PRIMARY    KEY
AUTO_INCREMENT,

    Studname VARCHAR(40) NOT NULL, DoB,

    phoneNum VARCHAR(25) NOT NULL UNIQUE

);
```

Constraints In SQL

As the name implies, it is a restriction or limitation imposed on a column (s) of a table in order to place a limitation on the type of values the table can store. They provide a better mechanism to retain the reliability and accuracy of the data contained in the table. We have several categories of constraints, which includes:

NOT NULL Constraint – This statement states that NULL values will not be accepted at the column. What it means is that a new row cannot be added in a table without the inclusion of a non-NULL value for such a column.

For instance, the statement below creates a table "studentRecords" with four columns and three of these columns (id, Studname, and phoneNum) do not accept NULL Values.

```
CREATE TABLE studentRecords (

    id INT NOT NULL,

    Studname VARCHAR(30) NOT NULL,

    DoB DATE,

    phoneNum VARCHAR(15) NOT NULL

);
```

Tip: A null value is not the same as blank, zero (0), or a zero-length character string. The meaning of a NULL is that there hasn't been any entry made in that field.

- PRIMARY KEY Constraint – *This classifies a column (s) with values that distinctively recognize a row in the table.*

You cannot have two rows simultaneously in a particular table having the same value for its primary key. The example below shows a SQL statement creating a table named "studentRecords" and identify the id column as the primary key.

```
CREATE TABLE studentRecords (

    id INT NOT NULL PRIMARY KEY,

    Studname VARCHAR(30) NOT NULL,

    DoB DATE,

    phoneNum VARCHAR(15) NOT NULL

);
```

- UNIQUE Constraint – *if you want to restrict a column (s) to contain unique values in a table, the UNIQUE statement is used. While the PRIMARY KEY and UNIQUE constraint enforce uniqueness in a table; however, the UNIQUE constraint is used when your goal is to enforce the exclusivity on a particular column (s). I will use our previous example to specify the phone column as unique. With this, the phone column won't allow duplicated values.*

```
CREATE TABLE studentRecords (

    id INT NOT NULL PRIMARY KEY,

    Studname VARCHAR(30) NOT NULL,
```

```
    DoB DATE,

    phoneNum VARCHAR(15) NOT NULL UNIQUE,

    country VARCHAR(30) NOT NULL DEFAULT
'England'

);
```

- *FOREIGN KEY Constraint – This* particular kind of constraint is a column (s) used to set up and implement a relationship among data in two different tables.
- CHECK constraint – *The purpose of this statement is to restrict values in a column. For instance, the range of student age column can be restricted by creating CHECK constraint, which allows values only 16 to 45. This hinders ages entered from exceeding the age range. Here is an example to illustrate it.*

```
CREATE TABLE studentRecords (

    stu_id INT NOT NULL PRIMARY KEY,

    stu_name VARCHAR(55) NOT NULL,

    stu_date DATE NOT NULL,

    age INT NOT NULL CHECK (age >= 16 AND age
<= 45),

    dept_id INT,
```

```
     FOREIGN   KEY   (dept_id)   REFERENCES
departments(dept_id)

);
```

Inserting Data in Tables

In previous examples, I created a table with the name "studentRecords" in our "studentFile" database. Now, we need to add information into the table. To do this, SQL has a unique keyword, which is the "INSERT INTO" statement.

Format:

INSERT INTO NameOfTable (columnA, columnB, columnC,…) VALUES (value1, value2, value3,…);

The syntax is self-explanatory but if you are unclear, the tableName is the name of your table. In our examples so far, we have used "studentRecords." However, the column1, column2, column3,… represents the name of the table columns with value1, value2, value3 the parallel values for the columns.

To insert records to our "studentRecords" table, we will use the following statement.

```
INSERT INTO studentRecords (FullName, Age,
Sex, PhoneNum) ;
```

```
VALUES ('Donald Williamson', '30', 'Male', '0722-
022569') ;
```

If you observe, there is no value inserted for the id field. Do you remember when we created the table (studentRecords), we mark the id field with an AUTO_INCREMENT flag. Let's add another record to our table.

```
INSERT INTO studentRecords (FullName, Age,
Sex, PhoneNum) ;

VALUES ('Jefferson Peterson', '45', 'Male', '0252-
027948') ;
```

Why don't you add another one?

```
INSERT INTO studentRecords (FullName, Age,
Sex, PhoneNum) ;

VALUES ('Mariah Lawson', '50', 'Female', '0722-
457906') ;
```

If you were to display the output of this table, it will look like this

id	FullName	Age	Sex	PhoneNum
1	Donald Williamson	30	Male	0722-022569
2	Jefferson Peterson	45	Male	0252-027948
3	Mariah Lawson	50	Female	0722-457906

Chapter 1 Creating a Database in SQL Server

Like I mentioned above, SQL databases are among the most used databases across the world. This is because of a number of reasons, for instance it is very easy to create. What you need is a graphical user interface program that comes freely like a SQL Server Management. With that in place, creating a database is easy and you can start entering your data in no time at all. Here is how:

- **Start by installing the software(SQL Server Management Studio) to your computer**

This is software that is freely available for Microsoft. It will allow you to gain access to and also to work with your SQL server from a graphical interface other than using a command line for the same. The software will also allow you to gain access to a remote request of an SQL server. If not this one, you will require a similar software.

There are other interfaces that are available for other platforms like Mac for instance SQuirreL SQL. Such interfaces may differ but they all work the same.

You can also create a database using the tools available in command line.

2. Once the software has been installed, start it up.

After the installation, you can now start your program. You will be required to choose if you want to connect to a certain server. If there is a server already that is already set and working and you have all the permissions connect access it, just enter its address and the authentication information. But if you want to build your own local database, you will create the Database name and the type of authentication under the **Windows Authentication**.

Chapter 1 Now locate your database folder

After a connection has been made to the server, whether it is a local connection or a remote one, the Object Explorer will now open on the left hand side of your screen. Right at the top part of your Object Explorer diagram, you will see the server that you are using to. If it has not been expanded, click on the "+" icon that is following it and it will expand.

1. You can now create a fresh database

Spot the database folder and right click on it. Click on New database option from the list that will come up. This will give you a new window which will allow you to organize your database before you start creating it. First of all, you need to give your database a new and unique name, which will make it easy for you to identify it. The other settings can be left just the way they are at default settings unless there is an important change that you want to make. When you give your database a name, there are two other additional files that will be formed automatically, which are log and data files. The data file will be the one that will host all your information in your database and the log file will be the one that will track all the changes that you will make on the database. When satisfied, you can hit OK in order to create your database. Your newly created database will now appear in the extended database Folder, with a cylindrical icon, it will be easy to spot it.

1. Start creating your table

You have to come up with a structure where you will start storing your data and this will be your table. With a table, you can hold all manner of information and data that you want stored in the database. This is an important part before you can go on. To do this, you enlarge the new database that is in your database folder and then right click on the table's icon to select a New Table option. Windows thereafter opens everything else on your screen to let you to work on your new table as much as you want.

• It's time for the primary key

Primary keys are very important, therefore it is important to let them be the first entry on the first column of your SQL table. They act as the ID number or the highest number that helps you quickly remember what you have put in record in that table. In order to create your primary keys, enter ID on the field that has the Column Name and enter INT into the field marked Data Type. As of the Allow Nulls, ensure that they are all unchecked. Now hit the key icon in your toolbar in order to make this column your primary key. With this, you will not have null values but if you want to have a null value as your principal entry, you will check to Allow Nulls.

Scroll down the column properties to find the option Identity Specification. Expanding this option and setting it to a YES will ensure that the values on the ID column increases automatically on every entry that you will make. With this, all your new entries will be effectively numbered in the right order.

4. It's time to understand how tables are designed

This is an important part so as to find it easy to enter information in your database. With tables, you will get different columns or fields and every column denotes an aspect of every database entry that you will make. If you have a database for people in an organization for instance, your will have a FirsName column entry, LastName column entry, Address, Phone Number and such like entries.

- ## The other columns

When all the fields of the Primary Key have been filled in, other fields will automatically form beneath it. These will be the fields where all your other data will be entered. You are now free to enter data in those fields the way you want to. The right data type has to be chosen though so that it will match the data that you have filled in that column.

nchar(#) represents the type of data that should be used for the text for instance addresses, names among others. In the parenthesis will be a number which is the highest number that will be allowed in that field. You can set the limit in order to allow the size of your database to remain manageable. You can for instance use this format for the phone numbers in order to make it hard for you to perform mathematical function on the numbers.

int on the other hand represents data in whole numbers. This is the one that is used in the field marked ID.

decimal(x,y) will save your numbers in a decimal format. The number within the parenthesis will signify the total number of numerals and the other number of digits that will follow the decimals respectively.

- **When all that is done, save the table**

First save the table then you can start entering information on your columns. To do this, click on the Save button on your toolbar, then enter the name for your table. It is important to have a unique and easy to understand name for your table so that you will be able to tell what the table is all about without going through the data in it. This will be very useful especially once you start using large databases that have so many tables.

Chapter 1 The SQL Structure

In this chapter you will learn the fundamental features of the SQL language and an overview of its programming aspect. In addition, you will be presented with a step-by-step instruction on where and how to download SQLite, a version of the SQL software that will be used all throughout the discussion of this e-Book.

SQL Fundamental Features

SQL is a flexible computer language that you can deploy in different ways to communicate with relational databases. This software has some distinct features that differentiates it from other programming applications. First and foremost, SQL is a nonprocedural language. Most computer programs (e.g., C, C++ and Java) solve problems by following a sequence of commands that is called a *procedure*. In this case, one specific operation is performed after another until the required task has been accomplished. The flow of operation can either be a linear sequence or a looping one, depending on what the programmer had specified. This is not the same for SQL. In using this application, you will just have to specify the output that you want, not how you want to generate the output. From the CUSTOMER TABLE, if you want to create a separate list of contacts whose company are located in Texas then you have to retrieve the rows where the STATE column contains "TX" as its value. In writing the SQL command, you don't have to indicate how the information should be retrieved. It is the primary role of the database management system to examine the database and decide how to generate the results you wanted.

Learning the SQL syntax is like understanding the English language structure. Its command language, comprised of a limited number of statements, performs three primary data functions - definition, manipulation and control. The SQL programming language also includes reserved words that are only to be used for specific purposes. Thus, you cannot use these words as names for variables, tables and columns; or in any other way apart from their intended use. Below are some of the most common reserved words in SQL:2011.

ABS	ALL	ALLOC ATE	ALTER	AND	ANY
ARE	ARRAY	AS	AT	AVG	BEGIN
BETWE EN	BINAR Y	BOOLE AN	BOTH	BY	CALL
CASCA DED	CASE	CEILIN G	CHAR	CHARA CTER	CHECK

CLOSE	COLLATE	COLLECT	COLUMN	COMMIT	CONDITION
CONNECT	CONSTRAINT	CONVERT	COUNT	CREATE	CURSOR
CYCLE	DATE	DAY	DEALLOCATE	DEC	DECIMAL
DECLARE	DEFAULT	DELETE	DESCRIBE	DISCONNECT	DISTINCT
DOUBLE	DROP	DYNAMIC	EACH	ELEMENT	ELSE
END	ESCAPE	EVERY	EXCEPT	EXECUTE	EXISTS
EXTERNAL	EXTRACT	FALSE	FETCH	FILTER	FLOAT
FLOOR	FOR	FOREVER	FREE	FROM	FULL
FUNCTION	FUSION	GET	GLOBAL	GRANT	GROUP
GROUPING	HAVING	HOLD	HOUR	HOURS	IDENTITY
IN	INNER	INOUT	INSERT	INT	INTEGER
INTERSECT	INTERVAL	INTO	IS	JOIN	KEEP
LANGUAGE	LARGE	LEAD	LEFT	LIKE	LOCAL
LOWER	MATCH	MAX	MEMBER	MERGE	METHOD

MINUTE	MOD	MODULE	MONTH	MULTISET	NATIONAL
NATURAL	NEW	NIL	NO	NONE	NORMALIZE
NOT	NULL	NUMERIC	OF	OFFSET	OLD
ON	ONLY	OPEN	OR	ORDER	OUT
OVER	OVERLAY	PARAMETER	PARTITION	POSITION	POWER
PRECISION	PREPARE	PRIMARY	PROCEDURE	RANGE	RANK
REAL	RECURSIVE	REF	REFERENCES	REFERENCING	RELEASE
RESULT	RETURN	REVOKE	RIGHT	ROLLBACK	ROLLUP
ROW	ROWS	SCOPE	SCROLL	SEARCH	SECOND
SELECT	SET	SIMILAR	SOME	SPECIFIC	SQL
START	STATIC	SUM	SYMMETRIC	SYSTEM	TABLE
THEN	TIME	TIMESTAMP	TO	TRANSLATE	TREAT
TRIGGER	TRUNCATE	TRIM	TRUE	UNION	UNIQUE
UNKNOWN	UPDATE	UPPER	USER	USING	VALUE

VALUES	VARCHAR	VARYING	VERSION	WHEN	WHENEVER
WHERE	WINDOW	WITH	WITHIN	WITHOUT	YEAR

If you think that an SQL database is just a collection of tables, then you are wrong. There are additional structures that need to be specified to maintain the integrity of your data, such as schemas, domains and constraints.

- *Schema* – This is also called the *conceptual view* or the *complete logical view* that defines the entire database structure and provides overall table organization. Such schema is considered a metadata – stored in tables and part of the database (just like tables that consist of regular data).

- *Domain* – This specifies the set of all finite data values you can store in a particular table column or attribute. For example, in our previous CUSTOMER TABLE the STATE column can only contain the values "TX", "NY", "CA" and "NV" if you only provide products and services in the states of Texas, New York, California and Nevada respectively. So these four state abbreviations are the domain of the STATE attribute.

• *Constraint* – Often ignored but one of the important database components, this sets down the rules that identify what data values a specific table attribute can contain. Incorporating tight constraints assures that database users only enter valid data into a particular column. Together with defined table characteristics, column constraints determine its domain. Using the same STATE column as an example with the given constraint of only the four values, if a database user enters "NJ" for New Jersey, then the entry will not be accepted. The system will not proceed until a valid value is entered for the STATE attribute, unless the database structure needs to be updated due to sudden business changes.

ROLLBACK [WORK];

In the previous command line, the keyword *WORK* is optional.

• *SAVEPOINT* – This statement works with the ROLLBACK command, wherein it creates sections or points within groups of transactions in which you will be performing the ROLLBACK command. Its syntax is:

SAVEPOINT *SAVEPOINT_NAME*;

SQLite Installation Instructions and Database Features

Before you start overwhelming yourself with various database solutions and SQL command lines, you need to determine first your purpose why you are creating a database. This will further determine other database design considerations such as size, complexity, type of machine where the application will run, storage medium and more. When you start thinking of your database requirements, you need to know up to what level of detail should be considered in your design. Too much detail will result to a very complex design that further wastes time and effort, and even your computer's storage space. Too little will lead to a poor performing, corrupt and worthless database. Once you are done with the design phase, then you can decide which database software you can download to start your SQL experience.

For the sake of this e-Book's discussion, SQLite, a simple software library, will be used as a starter database engine to design, build and deploy applications. A free and stand-alone database software that is quick to download and easy to administer, SQLite was developed by Richard Hipp and his team of programmers. It is was designed so that it can be easily configured and implemented, which does not require any client-server setup at all.

Thus, SQLite is considered as one of the most widely used database software applications in the world.

Stated below are some of the major features of SQLite:

- Transactions are atomic, consistent, isolated and durable
- Compilation is simple and easy
- System crashes and power failures are supported
- Full SQL implementation with a stand-alone command-line interface client
- Code footprint is significantly small
- Adaptable and adjustable to larger projects
- Self-contained with no external dependencies
- *Portable and supports other platforms like Windows, Android, iOS, Mac, Solaris and more*

In using SQLite, you need to download *SQLiteStudio* as your database manager and editor. With its intuitive interface, this software is very light yet fast and powerful. You don't even need to install it, just download, unpack and run the application. Follow these simple steps in downloading SQLiteStudio on a Windows 10 computer:

- Go to http://sqlitestudio.pl/?act=about. You should get the following page:

2.   Check the version of your computer's operating system then click the appropriate link to start downloading the software.

After downloading the software, go to the folder where the application was saved (usually the Downloads Folder in Windows). Click on the *Extract* tab on top then choose the *Extract all* option.

You will get the *Extract Compressed (Zipped) Folders* dialog box. Change the destination folder to C:\SQL then click the *Extract* button. This will be the folder where all your SQLite files will be saved.

Chapter 1 Once all the files have been extracted, you will have the SQLiteStudio subfolder.

• Find the application program named SQLiteStudio inside the subfolder. To create a shortcut on your desktop (so you can quickly launch the application), right-click the filename, select *Send to* option then choose *Desktop (create shortcut)*.

7.   When you double-click the SQLiteStudio icon on your desktop,

• you should get the following screen:

Chapter 2 Database Administration

Once you have your database up and running with tables and queries it is up you to keep the production database running smoothly. The database will have to be regularly looked at in order to ensure that it continues to perform as originally intended. If a database is poorly maintained it can easily result in a website connected to it performing poorly or worse still result in down time or even data loss. There is usually a person designated to look after the database and their job is titled Database Administrator or DBA. However, it's usually a non-DBA person who needs help with the database.

There are a number of different tasks which you can perform when carrying out maintenance which include the following:

Database Integrity: When you check the integrity of the database you are running checks on the data to make sure that both the physical and logical structure of the database is consistent and accurate.

Index Reorganization: Once you start to insert and delete data on your database there is going to be fragmentation (or a scattering) of indexes. Reorganizing the index will bring everything back together again and increase speed.

Rebuild Index: You don't have to perform an index reorganization, you can drop an index and then recreate them.

Database Backup: One of the most important tasks to perform. There are a number of different ways in which you can back up the database, these include: Full which backs up the database entirely, Differential which backs up the database since the last full backup and Transaction log which only backs up the transactional log.

Check Database Statistics: You can check the statistics of the database which are kept on queries. If you update the statistics, which can get out of date, you can help aid the queries being run.

Data and Log File: In general, make sure the data and log files are kept separate from each other. These files will grow when your database is being used and its best to allocate them an appropriate size going forward (and not just enable them to grow).

Depending on your database some tasks may be more useful than others. Apart from database backup which probably mandatory if it's in production you can pick through the other tasks depending on the state of the database.

For example, should the fragmentation of the database be below 30% then you can choose to perform an index reorganization. However, if the database fragmentation is greater than 30% then you should rebuild the index. You can rebuild the index on a weekly basis or more often if possible.

You can run a maintenance plan on SQL Server via its Server Agent depending on database requirements. It's important to set the times right not when your application is expected to be busy. You can choose a time or you can run it when the server CPU is not busy. Choosing to run when the server is not busy is a more preferred option for larger databases than selecting a particular time as there is no guaranteed time which the CPU will be idle. However, it is usually only a concern if your application is quite big and has a lot of requests.

When you do rebuild the indexes, it is important that you have the results sorted in tempdb. When using tempdb the old indexes are kept until new ones are added. Normally rebuilding the indexes uses the fixed space which the database was allocated. So, if you run out of disk space then you would not be able to complete the rebuilding of indexes. It's possible to use the tempdb and not have to increase the database disk size. The database maintenance can be run both synchronous (wait for task completion) or asynchronous (together) to speed things up however you must make sure that the tasks run in the right order.

Setting up a maintenance plan in SQL Server

To set up a maintenance plan in SQL Server you first must get the server to show advanced options. This is done by running the following code in a new query in SQL Server:

sp_configure 'show advanced options', 1

GO

RECONFIGURE

GO

sp_configure 'Agent XPs', 1

GO

RECONFIGURE

GO

SQL Server will now display the advanced options. Left click the + icon to the left of Management which is on the left-hand side of SQL Server Management Studio. Now left click Maintenance Plans and then right click Maintenance Plans. Select New Maintenance Plan Wizard.

Enter an appropriate maintenance plan name and description. From here you can either run one or all tasks in one plan and have as many plans as you want. After you have given a name, choose single schedule and click next.

You will see a number of options which you can pick for your maintenance including: *Check Database Integrity, Shrink Database, Reorganize Index, Rebuild Index, Update Statistics, Clean up History, Execute SQL Server Agent Job, Back Up – full, differential or transaction log and Maintenance Cleanup Task*. Select which you want to perform (in this example select all) This wizard will bring you through each of the items you have selected to fine tune them.

Once you select the items you want in your plan click next, you can now rearrange them in the order you wish them to complete. It's best to have Database Backup first in case of power failure, so select it and move it to the top of the list. Click next.

Define Back Up Database (Full) Task

This screen allows you to pick which full database backup you wish to perform it on. Best practice is to keep one plan per database, select one database and select next.

Define Database Check Integrity Task

This screen – the integrity task is a SQL Server command which checks the integrity of the database to see if everything is not corrupt and stable. Select a database and click next.

Define Shrink Database Task

You can now configure to shrink the database in order to free up space in the next screen. It will only shrink space if available but should you need space in the future you will have to re allocate it. However, this step will help backup speeds. Most developers don't use this feature that much. Click next after selecting a database to shrink.

Define Reorganize Index Task

The next screen is the Define Reorganize Index Tag screen. When you add, modify and delete indexes you will, like tables, need to reorganize them. The process is the same as a hard disk where you have there are fragmented files and space scattered across the disk. Best practice is to perform this task once per week for a busy database. You can choose to compact large object which compacts any index which has large binary object data. Click next to proceed to the next screen.

Define Rebuild Index Task

This screen covers individual index rows. As mentioned either reorganize or reindexing. Doing both together in one plan is pointless. Depending on your fragmentation level pick one or the other. In this example select your database and sort results in tempdb. Click next to proceed.

Define Update Statistics Task

The update statistics task helps developer keep track of data retrieval as its created, modified and deleted. You can keep the statistics up to date by performing this plan. Both statistics for index and statistics for individual columns are kept. Select your database and click next to proceed.

Define History Cleanup Task

You should now see the Define maintenance cleanup task screen which specifies the historical data to delete. You can specify a shorter time frame to keep the backup and recovery, agent job history and maintenance place for on the drop down. Click next to proceed.

Define Back up Database (Differential) Task

This screen allows you to back up every page in the database which has been changed since the last full backup. Select a database you wish to use and click next.

Define Back Up Database (Transaction Log) Task

The transaction log backup backs up all the log records since the last backup. You can choose a folder to store it. Performing this type of backup is the least resource intensive backup. Select a database and storage location and click next.

Define Execute SQL Server Agent Job Task

The SQL Server Agent Job Task deals with jobs that are outside the wizard, for example it could be to check for nulls, check whether the database meets specified standards etc. Any jobs that are specified in SQL Server Agent Job Task are listed here. Click next to proceed.

Define Maintenance Cleanup Task

This screen defines the clean-up action of the maintenance task i.e. to ensure that the they are not taking up unnecessary space, so you can specify where to store them. You can delete specific backup files. Click next to proceed.

Report Options

The next screen covers where you want to store the report of the maintenance plan. Make a note of where you are going to store it. You need to have email set up on SQL Server in order to email it. Click next to proceed.

Complete the Wizard

The final screen is a complete review of the wizard. You can review the summary of the plan and which options were selected. Clicking finishes ends the wizard and creates the plan. You should now see a success screen with the tasks completed.

Running the maintenance plan

Once you successfully complete the maintenance wizard the next step is to run the plan you created. In order to get the plan to run you need to have the SQL Server Agent running. It is visible two down from where Management is on SQL Server Management Studio. You can left click SQL Server Agent and then right click and select Start.

Also, you can press the windows key + and press the letter r, then type in services.msc and hit return. Once Services appear scroll down and look for SQL Server Agent (MSSQLEXPRESS). SQL Server Express was installed in this EBook but you can select the other versions like (MSSQLSERVER) if you installed that. Left click it, then right click it and select Start.

You can go back to SSMS and right click on the maintenance plan you created under maintenance plans and then select Execute. This will now run your plan. One successful completion of the plan click ok and close the dialogue box. You can view the reports by right clicking the maintenance plan you created and selecting View history. On the left-hand side are all the different plans in SQL Server while on the right is the results of the specific plan.

Emailing the reports.

A lot of DBA's like to get their database reports via email. What you need to do is to set up a database mail before you can fire off emails and then set up a Server agent to send the email.

Setting up Database Mail.

The first step is to right click Database mail in SSMS and select configure database mail. A wizard screen will appear, click next. Now select the first choice – set up Database Mail and click next. Enter a profile name optional description of the profile. Now click on the Add button to the right.

This will bring you to an add New Database Mail Account – SMTP. You need to enter the STMP details for an email account. Maybe you can set up a new email account for this service. You can search online for SMTP details, Gmail works quite well (server name: smtp.gmail.com, port number 587, SSL required, tick basic authentication & confirm password). Click on ok. Click next, click on public (important: so it can be used by the rest of the database). Set it as default profile, click next, click next again. You should now get a success screen. Click close.

Possible Error: It is important to ensure you select yes to public profile when you are at the Manage Profile Security part of the wizard above. If there is no public profile – no emails can be sent. You can check by running the following in a new query and check to ensure

SQL Server Agent

To send off the database email you need to set up a Server Agent. Start by right clicking on SQL Server

Agent – New – Operator. Give the operator a name like Maintenance Plan Operator and enter in the email address you wish to send the report to and click ok.

Now right the maintenance plan that you have successfully executed and select modify. The maintenance plan design screen will appear on the right-hand side where you can see some graphics of the tasks completed in it. Now click on Reporting and Logging – it is an icon situated on the menu bar of the design plan -   to the left of Manage Connections…

The Reporting and Logging window will appear. Select the tick box – Send report to an email recipient and select the Maintenance plan operator you just created. The next time you run the plan an email will be sent to the email address.

Summary

The running and maintenance of a database is an important job. Having the right plan for your database means it will continue to work as originally designed and you can quickly identify database errors or slowdowns early on and fix them quickly.

Chapter 3 Structure of the SELECT Statement

The SELECT Clause

The SELECT clause is the only required clause in a SELECT statement, all the other clauses are optional. The SELECT columns can be literals (constants), expressions, table columns and even subqueries. Lines can be commented with "--".

```
SELECT                    15                    *
15;                                          -- 225

SELECT      Today      =      convert(DATE,
getdate());          -- 2016-07-27

SELECT                    Color,

            ProdCnt                    =
COUNT(*),

            AvgPrice                   =
FORMAT(AVG(ListPrice),'c','en-US')

FROM AdventureWorks2012.Production.Product p

WHERE Color is not null

GROUP BY Color   HAVING count(*) > 10

ORDER BY AvgPrice DESC;
```

GO

Color	ProdCnt	AvgPrice
Yellow	36	$959.09
Blue	26	$923.68
Silver	43	$850.31
Black	93	$725.12
Red	38	$1,401.95

-- Equivalent with column aliases on the right

```
SELECT                    Color,

            COUNT(*)
            AS ProdCnt,

                FORMAT(AVG(ListPrice),'c','en-
US')        AS AvgPrice

FROM AdventureWorks2012.Production.Product p

WHERE Color is not null  GROUP BY Color

HAVING count(*) > 10

ORDER BY AvgPrice DESC;

GO
```

SELECT with Search Expression

SELECT statement can have complex expressions for text or numbers as demonstrated in the next T-SQL query for finding the street name in AddressLine1 column.

```
SELECT            AddressID,

          SUBSTRING(AddressLine1,
CHARINDEX(' ', AddressLine1+' ', 1) +1,

          CHARINDEX(' ', AddressLine1+' ',
CHARINDEX(' ', AddressLine1+' ', 1) +1) -

          CHARINDEX(' ', AddressLine1+' ', 1)
-
1)
AS StreetName,

              AddressLine1,

        City

FROM AdventureWorks2012.Person.Address

WHERE ISNUMERIC (LEFT(AddressLine1,1))=1

  AND City = 'Seattle'

ORDER BY AddressLine1;

-- -- (141 row(s) affected)- Partial results.
```

AddressID	StreetName	AddressLine1	City
13079	boulevard	081, boulevard du Montparnasse	Seattle
859	Oak	1050 Oak Street	Seattle
110	Slow	1064 Slow Creek Road	Seattle
113	Ravenwood	1102 Ravenwood	Seattle
95	Bradford	1220 Bradford Way	Seattle
32510	Steven	1349 Steven Way	Seattle
118	Balboa	136 Balboa Court	Seattle
32519	Mazatlan	137 Mazatlan	Seattle
25869	Calle	1386 Calle Verde	Seattle
114	Yorba	1398 Yorba Linda	Seattle
15657	Book	151 Book Ct	Seattle
105	Stillman	1619 Stillman Court	Seattle
18002	Carmel	1635 Carmel Dr	Seattle
19813	Acardia	1787 Acardia Pl.	Seattle
16392	Orchid	1874 Orchid Ct	Seattle

18053	Green	1883 Green View Court	Seattle
13035	Mt.	1887 Mt. Diablo St	Seattle
29864	Valley	1946 Valley Crest Drive	Seattle
13580	Hill	2030 Hill Drive	Seattle
106	San	2144 San Rafael	Seattle

SELECT Statement with Subquery

Two Northwind category images, Beverages & Dairy Products, from the dbo.Categories table.

The following SELECT statement involves a subquery which is called a derived table. It also demonstrates that INNER JOIN can be performed with a GROUP BY subquery as well not only with another table or view.

```sql
USE Northwind;

SELECT          c.CategoryName
                          AS Category,

                cnum.NoOfProducts
                AS CatProdCnt,

                      p.ProductName
                      AS Product,

                      FORMAT(p.UnitPrice,'c',
'en-US')              AS UnitPrice

 FROM     Categories c

                          INNER JOIN Products p

                                      ON
c.CategoryID = p.CategoryID

                          INNER    JOIN
(          SELECT          c.CategoryID,


      NoOfProducts = count(* )

                                      FROM
  Categories c

                                      I
NNER JOIN Products p
```

```
                                      ON c.CategoryID = p.CategoryID

                                                                GROUP
BY c.CategoryID

                                                                    )
cnum                                                               --
derived table

                                                                   ON
c.CategoryID = cnum.CategoryID

ORDER BY Category, Product;

-- (77 row(s) affected) - Partial results.
```

Category	CatProdCnt	Product	UnitPrice
Dairy Products	10	Mozzarella di Giovanni	$34.80
Dairy Products	10	Queso Cabrales	$21.00
Dairy Products	10	Queso Manchego La Pastora	$38.00
Dairy Products	10	Raclette Courdavault	$55.00

Grains/Cereals	7	Filo Mix	$7.00
Grains/Cereals	7	Gnocchi di nonna Alice	$38.00
Grains/Cereals	7	Gustaf's Knäckebröd	$21.00
Grains/Cereals	7	Ravioli Angelo	$19.50
Grains/Cereals	7	Singaporean Hokkien Fried Mee	$14.00
Grains/Cereals	7	Tunnbröd	$9.00

Creating Delimited String List (CSV) with XML PATH

The XML PATH clause , the text() function and correlated subquery is used to create a comma delimited string within the SELECT columns. Note: it cannot be done using traditional (without XML) SQL single statement, it can be done with multiple SQL statements only. STUFF() string function is applied to replace the leading comma with an empty string

USE AdventureWorks;

```sql
SELECT          Territory          = st.[Name],

                                   SalesYTD
=    FORMAT(floor(SalesYTD),   'c',   'en-US'),   --
currency format

              SalesStaffAssignmentHistory =

              STUFF((SELECT    CONCAT(',    ',
c.FirstName,    SPACE(1),    c.LastName)          AS
[text()]

                    FROM   Person.Contact
c

                    INNER        JOIN
Sales.SalesTerritoryHistory sth

                    ON    c.ContactID    =
sth.SalesPersonID

                    WHERE  sth.TerritoryI
D =    st.TerritoryID

                    ORDER  BY StartDate

                    FOR XML Path ('')), 1,
1, SPACE(0))

FROM   Sales.SalesTerritory st

ORDER  BY SalesYTD DESC;

GO
```

Territory	SalesYTD	SalesStaffAssignmentHistory
Southwest	$8,351,296.00	Shelley Dyck, Jauna Elson
Canada	$6,917,270.00	Carla Eldridge, Michael Emanuel, Gail Erickson
Northwest	$5,767,341.00	Shannon Elliott, Terry Eminhizer, Martha Espinoza
Central	$4,677,108.00	Linda Ecoffey, Maciej Dusza
France	$3,899,045.00	Mark Erickson
Northeast	$3,857,163.00	Maciej Dusza, Linda Ecoffey
United Kingdom	$3,514,865.00	Michael Emanuel
Southeast	$2,851,419.00	Carol Elliott
Germany	$2,481,039.00	Janeth Esteves
Australia	$1,977,474.00	Twanna Evans

Logical Processing Order of the SELECT Statement

The results from the previous step will be available to the next step. The logical processing order for a SELECT statement is the following. Actual processing by the database engine may be different due to performance and other considerations.

1. FROM

2. ON

3. JOIN

4. WHERE

5. GROUP BY

6. WITH CUBE or WITH ROLLUP

7. HAVING

8. SELECT

9. DISTINCT

10. ORDER BY

11. TOP

As an example, it is logical to filter with the WHERE clause prior to applying GROUP BY. It is also logical to sort when the final result set is available.

SELECT Color, COUNT(*) AS ColorCount FROM AdventureWorks2012.Production.Product

WHERE Color is not NULL GROUP BY Color ORDER BY ColorCount DESC;

Color	ColorCount
Black	93
Silver	43
Red	38

Yellow	36
Blue	26
Multi	8
Silver/Black	7
White	4
Grey	1

The TOP Clause

The TOP clause filters results according the sorting specified in an ORDER BY clause, otherwise random filtering takes place.

Simple TOP usage to return 10 rows only.

SELECT TOP 10 SalesOrderID, OrderDate, TotalDue

FROM
AdventureWorks2012.Sales.SalesOrderHeader   OR DER BY TotalDue DESC;

SalesOrderID	OrderDate	TotalDue
51131	2007-07-01 00:00:00.000	187487.825
55282	2007-10-01 00:00:00.000	182018.6272
46616	2006-07-01 00:00:00.000	170512.6689

46981	2006-08-01 00:00:00.000	166537.0808
47395	2006-09-01 00:00:00.000	165028.7482
47369	2006-09-01 00:00:00.000	158056.5449
47355	2006-09-01 00:00:00.000	145741.8553
51822	2007-08-01 00:00:00.000	145454.366
44518	2005-11-01 00:00:00.000	142312.2199
51858	2007-08-01 00:00:00.000	140042.1209

Complex TOP function usage: not known in advance how many rows will be returned due to "TIES".

```
SELECT    TOP  1  WITH  TIES   coalesce(Color,
'N/A')                         AS Color,

          FORMAT(ListPrice,    'c',    'en-
US')                           AS ListPrice,

          Name
                    AS ProductName,

          ProductID

FROM    AdventureWorks2012.Production.Product
```

ORDER BY ROW_NUMBER() OVER(PARTITION BY Color ORDER BY ListPrice DESC);

Color	ListPrice	ProductName	ProductID
N/A	$229.49	HL Fork	804
Black	$3,374.99	Mountain-100 Black, 38	775
Red	$3,578.27	Road-150 Red, 62	749
Silver	$3,399.99	Mountain-100 Silver, 38	771
Blue	$2,384.07	Touring-1000 Blue, 46	966
Grey	$125.00	Touring-Panniers, Large	842
Multi	$89.99	Men's Bib-Shorts, S	855
Silver/Black	$80.99	HL Mountain Pedal	937
White	$9.50	Mountain Bike Socks, M	709
Yellow	$2,384.07	Touring-1000 Yellow, 46	954

The DISTINCT Clause to Omit Duplicates

The DISTINCT clause returns only unique results, omitting duplicates in the result set.

USE AdventureWorks2012;

SELECT DISTINCT Color FROM Production.Product

WHERE Color is not NULL

ORDER BY Color;

GO

Color
Black
Blue
Grey
Multi
Red
Silver
Silver/Black
White
Yellow

```sql
SELECT DISTINCT ListPrice

FROM Production.Product

 WHERE ListPrice > 0.0

ORDER BY ListPrice DESC;

GO

-- (102 row(s) affected) - Partial results.
```

ListPrice
3578.27
3399.99
3374.99
2443.35

```sql
-- Using DISTINCT in COUNT - NULL is counted
SELECT                    COUNT(*)
            AS TotalRows,

                          COUNT(DISTINCT
Color)             AS ProductColors,

                          COUNT(DISTINCT
Size)              AS ProductSizes
```

FROM AdventureWorks2012.Production.Product;

TotalRows	ProductColors	ProductSizes
504	9	18

-

The CASE Conditional Expression

The CASE conditional expression evaluates to a single value of the same data type, therefore it can be used anywhere in a query where a single value is required.

SELECT   CASE ProductLine

                              WHEN 'R' THEN
'Road'

                              WHEN 'M' THEN
'Mountain'

                              WHEN 'T' THEN
'Touring'

                              WHEN 'S' THEN
'Other'

                              ELSE 'Parts'

                    END
            AS Category,

```
            Name
        AS ProductName,

        ProductNumber

FROM AdventureWorks2012.Production.Product

ORDER BY ProductName;

GO

-- (504 row(s) affected) - Partial results.
```

Category	ProductName	ProductNumber
Touring	Touring-3000 Blue, 62	BK-T18U-62
Touring	Touring-3000 Yellow, 44	BK-T18Y-44
Touring	Touring-3000 Yellow, 50	BK-T18Y-50
Touring	Touring-3000 Yellow, 54	BK-T18Y-54
Touring	Touring-3000 Yellow, 58	BK-T18Y-58
Touring	Touring-3000 Yellow, 62	BK-T18Y-62
Touring	Touring-Panniers, Large	PA-T100
Other	Water Bottle - 30 oz.	WB-H098
Mountain	Women's Mountain Shorts, L	SH-W890-L

Query to return different result sets for repeated execution due to newid().

```
SELECT                TOP                3
CompanyName,      City=CONCAT(City,    ',    ',
Country),              PostalCode,

        [IsNumeric] =   CASE              WHEN
PostalCode like '[0-9][0-9][0-9][0-9][0-9]'

                                          THEN
'5-Digit Numeric'    ELSE 'Other'  END

FROM    Northwind.dbo.Suppliers

ORDER BY NEWID();                          -
- random sort

GO
```

CompanyName	City	PostalCode	IsNumeric
PB Knäckebröd AB	Göteborg, Sweden	S-345 67	Other
Gai pâturage	Annecy, France	74000	5-Digit Numeric
Heli Süßwaren GmbH & Co. KG	Berlin, Germany	10785	5-Digit Numeric

Same query as above expanded with ROW_NUMBER() and another CASE expression column.

```
SELECT        ROW_NUMBER() OVER (ORDER
BY Name)              AS RowNo,

              CASE ProductLine

                   WHEN 'R' THEN 'Road'

                        WHEN 'M' THEN
'Mountain'

                   WHEN 'T' THEN 'Touring'

                   WHEN 'S' THEN 'Other'

                   ELSE 'Parts'

              END
                 AS Category,

              Name
                 AS ProductName,

              CASE WHEN Color is null THEN
'N/A'

                             ELSE   Color
END                         AS Color,

              ProductNumber
```

FROM   Production.Product   ORDER   BY
ProductName;

-- (504 row(s) affected) - Partial results.

RowNo	Category	ProductName	Color	ProductNumber
1	Parts	Adjustable Race	N/A	AR-5381
2	Mountain	All-Purpose Bike Stand	N/A	ST-1401
3	Other	AWC Logo Cap	Multi	CA-1098
4	Parts	BB Ball Bearing	N/A	BE-2349
5	Parts	Bearing Ball	N/A	BA-8327
6	Other	Bike Wash - Dissolver	N/A	CL-9009
7	Parts	Blade	N/A	BL-2036
8	Other	Cable Lock	N/A	LO-C100
9	Parts	Chain	Silver	CH-0234
10	Parts	Chain Stays	N/A	CS-2812

Testing PostalCode with ISNUMERIC and generating a flag with CASE expression.

```
SELECT   TOP (4)
AddressID,   City,   PostalCode
                        AS Zip,
                CASE WHEN
ISNUMERIC(PostalCode) = 1 THEN 'Y'  ELSE
'N'  END                 AS IsZipNumeric
    FROM   AdventureWorks2008.Person.Address
ORDER BY NEWID();
```

AddressID	City	Zip	IsZipNumeric
16704	Paris	75008	Y
26320	Grossmont	91941	Y
27705	Matraville	2036	Y
18901	Kirkby	KB9	N

The OVER Clause

The OVER clause defines the partitioning and sorting of a rowset (intermediate result set) preceding the application of an associated window function, such as ranking. Window functions are also dubbed as ranking functions.

USE AdventureWorks2012;

```sql
-- Query with three different OVER clauses

SELECT          ROW_NUMBER() OVER ( ORDER
BY                            SalesOrderID,
ProductID)                             AS
RowNum

    ,SalesOrderID, ProductID, OrderQty

        ,RANK()     OVER(PARTITION     BY
SalesOrderID      ORDER      BY      OrderQty
DESC)              AS Ranking

        ,SUM(OrderQty) OVER(PARTITION BY
SalesOrderID)
   AS TotalQty

        ,AVG(OrderQty) OVER(PARTITION BY
SalesOrderID)
   AS AvgQty

        ,COUNT(OrderQty) OVER(PARTITION
BY SalesOrderID) AS "Count"  -- T-SQL keyword,
use "" or []

        ,MIN(OrderQty) OVER(PARTITION BY
SalesOrderID)
   AS "Min"

        ,MAX(OrderQty) OVER(PARTITION BY
SalesOrderID)
   AS "Max"
```

FROM Sales.SalesOrderDetail

WHERE SalesOrderID BETWEEN 61190 AND 61199 ORDER BY RowNum;

-- (143 row(s) affected) - Partial results.

Row Num m	Sales OrderI D	Prod uctI D	Ord erQt y	Ran kin g	Tot alQt y	Av gQ ty	Co un t	M i n	M a x
1	61190	707	4	13	159	3	40	1	1 7
2	61190	708	3	18	159	3	40	1	1 7
3	61190	711	5	8	159	3	40	1	1 7
4	61190	712	12	2	159	3	40	1	1 7
5	61190	714	3	18	159	3	40	1	1 7
6	61190	715	5	8	159	3	40	1	1 7
7	61190	716	5	8	159	3	40	1	1 7
8	61190	858	4	13	159	3	40	1	1 7

9	61190	859	7	6	159	3	40	1	17
10	61190	864	8	4	159	3	40	1	17
11	61190	865	3	18	159	3	40	1	17
12	61190	870	9	3	159	3	40	1	17
13	61190	876	4	13	159	3	40	1	17
14	61190	877	5	8	159	3	40	1	17
15	61190	880	1	34	159	3	40	1	17
16	61190	881	5	8	159	3	40	1	17
17	61190	883	2	26	159	3	40	1	17
18	61190	884	17	1	159	3	40	1	17
19	61190	885	3	18	159	3	40	1	17
20	61190	886	1	34	159	3	40	1	17
21	61190	889	2	26	159	3	40	1	17

22	61190	892	4	13	159	3	40	1	17
23	61190	893	3	18	159	3	40	1	17
24	61190	895	1	34	159	3	40	1	17

-

FROM Clause: Specifies the Data Source

The FROM clause specifies the source data sets for the query such as tables, views, derived tables and table-valued functions. Typically the tables are JOINed together. The most common JOIN is INNER JOIN which is based on equality between FOREIGN KEY and PRIMARY KEY values in the two tables.

PERFORMANCE NOTE

All FOREIGN KEYs should be indexed. PRIMARY KEYs are indexed automatically with unique index.

USE AdventureWorks2012;

GO

SELECT

```sql
    ROW_NUMBER()   OVER(ORDER   BY   SalesYTD
DESC)                                              AS
RowNo,

  ROW_NUMBER() OVER(PARTITION BY PostalCode
ORDER BY SalesYTD DESC)              AS SeqNo,

                        CONCAT(p.FirstName,
SPACE(1),   p.LastName)                            AS
SalesStaff,

                        FORMAT(s.SalesYTD,'c','en-
US')                                               AS
YTDSales,

                City,

                a.PostalCode
                                       AS ZipCode

FROM Sales.SalesPerson AS s

    INNER JOIN Person.Person AS p

      ON s.BusinessEntityID = p.BusinessEntityID

    INNER JOIN Person.Address AS a

      ON a.AddressID = p.BusinessEntityID

WHERE          TerritoryID IS NOT NULL   AND
SalesYTD <> 0 ORDER BY ZipCode, SeqNo;
```

RowNo	SeqNo	SalesStaff	YTDSales	City	ZipCode
1	1	Linda Mitchell	$4,251,368.55	Issaquah	98027
3	2	Michael Blythe	$3,763,178.18	Issaquah	98027
4	3	Jillian Carson	$3,189,418.37	Issaquah	98027
8	4	Tsvi Reiter	$2,315,185.61	Issaquah	98027
12	5	Garrett Vargas	$1,453,719.47	Issaquah	98027
14	6	Pamela Ansman-Wolfe	$1,352,577.13	Issaquah	98027
2	1	Jae Pak	$4,116,871.23	Renton	98055
5	2	Ranjit Varkey Chudukatil	$3,121,616.32	Renton	98055
6	3	José Saraiva	$2,604,540.72	Renton	98055
7	4	Shu Ito	$2,458,535.62	Renton	98055
9	5	Rachel Valdez	$1,827,066.71	Renton	98055

10	6	Tete Mensa-Annan	$1,576,562.20	Renton	98055
11	7	David Campbell	$1,573,012.94	Renton	98055
13	8	Lynn Tsoflias	$1,421,810.92	Renton	98055

The WHERE Clause to Filter Records (Rows)

The WHERE clause filters the rows generated by the query. Only rows satisfying (TRUE) the WHERE clause predicates are returned.

PERFORMANCE NOTE
All columns in WHERE clause should be indexed.

USE AdventureWorks2012;

String equal match predicate - equal is TRUE, not equal is FALSE.

SELECT ProductID, Name, ListPrice, Color

FROM Production.Product WHERE Name = 'Mountain-100 Silver, 38' ;

ProductID	Name	ListPrice	Color
771	Mountain-100 Silver, 38	3399.99	Silver

-- Function equality predicate

SELECT * FROM Sales.SalesOrderHeader WHERE YEAR(OrderDate) = 2008;

-- (13951 row(s) affected)

```
PERFORMANCE NOTE
When a column is used as a parameter in
  a function ( e.g. YEAR(OrderDate) ),
  index (if any) usage is voided.
Instead of random SEEK, all rows are
  SCANned in the table.  The predicate is
  not SARGable.
```

-- String wildcard match predicate

SELECT ProductID, Name, ListPrice, Color

FROM Production.Product WHERE Name LIKE ('%touring%');

-- Integer range predicate

SELECT ProductID, Name, ListPrice, Color

```
FROM  Production.Product  WHERE  ProductID  >=
997 ;
```

-- Double string wildcard match predicate

```
SELECT ProductID, Name, ListPrice, Color
```

```
FROM   Production.Product   WHERE   Name   LIKE
('%bike%')  AND Name LIKE ('%44%');
```

-- String list match predicate

```
SELECT ProductID, Name, ListPrice, Color  FROM
Production.Product
```

```
WHERE   Name   IN   ('Mountain-100   Silver,   44',
'Mountain-100 Black, 44');
```

The GROUP BY Clause to Aggregate Results

The GROUP BY clause is applied to partition the rows and calculate aggregate values. An extremely powerful way of looking at the data from a summary point of view.

```
SELECT

                    V.Name
                                    AS Vendor,

                    FORMAT(SUM(TotalDue),  'c',
'en-US')                    AS TotalPurchase,

                A.City,
```

```sql
        SP.Name
            AS State,

    CR.Name
            AS Country

FROM Purchasing.Vendor AS V

    INNER JOIN Purchasing.VendorAddress AS VA

            ON VA.VendorID = V.VendorID

    INNER JOIN Person.Address AS A

            ON A.AddressID = VA.AddressID

    INNER JOIN Person.StateProvince AS SP

            ON   SP.StateProvinceID
=   A.StateProvinceID

    INNER JOIN Person.CountryRegion AS CR

            ON  CR.CountryRegionCode  =
SP.CountryRegionCode

    INNER  JOIN  Purchasing.PurchaseOrderHeader
POH

            ON   POH.VendorID   =
V.VendorID

GROUP BY  V.Name, A.City, SP.Name, CR.Name
```

ORDER BY SUM(TotalDue) DESC, Vendor; -- TotalPurchase does a string sort instead of numeric

GO

-- (79 row(s) affected) - Partial results.

Vendor	TotalPurchase	City	State	Country
Superior Bicycles	$5,034,266.74	Lynnwood	Washington	United States
Professional Athletic Consultants	$3,379,946.32	Burbank	California	United States
Chicago City Saddles	$3,347,165.20	Daly City	California	United States
Jackson Authority	$2,821,333.52	Long Beach	California	United States
Vision Cycles, Inc.	$2,777,684.91	Glendale	California	United States

Sport Fan Co.	$2,675,889.22	Burien	Washington	United States
Proseware, Inc.	$2,593,901.31	Lebanon	Oregon	United States
Crowley Sport	$2,472,770.05	Chicago	Illinois	United States
Greenwood Athletic Company	$2,472,770.05	Lemon Grove	Arizona	United States
Mitchell Sports	$2,424,284.37	Everett	Washington	United States
First Rate Bicycles	$2,304,231.55	La Mesa	New Mexico	United States
Signature Cycles	$2,236,033.80	Coronado	California	United States

Electronic Bike Repair & Supplies	$2,154,773.37	Tacoma	Washington	United States
Vista Road Bikes	$2,090,857.52	Salem	Oregon	United States
Victory Bikes	$2,052,173.62	Issaquah	Washington	United States
Bicycle Specialists	$1,952,375.30	Lake Oswego	Oregon	United States

The HAVING Clause to Filter Aggregates

The HAVING clause is similar to the WHERE clause filtering but applies to GROUP BY aggregates.

USE AdventureWorks;

SELECT

V.Name
AS Vendor,

FORMAT(SUM(TotalDue), 'c', 'en-US')   AS TotalPurchase,

```sql
        A.City,

        SP.Name
AS State,

        CR.Name
AS Country

FROM Purchasing.Vendor AS V

    INNER JOIN Purchasing.VendorAddress AS VA

            ON VA.VendorID = V.VendorID

    INNER JOIN Person.Address AS A

            ON A.AddressID = VA.AddressID

    INNER JOIN Person.StateProvince AS SP

                ON   SP.StateProvinceID
=   A.StateProvinceID

    INNER JOIN Person.CountryRegion AS CR

            ON CR.CountryRegionCode =
SP.CountryRegionCode

    INNER JOIN Purchasing.PurchaseOrderHeader
POH

                ON  POH.VendorID  =
V.VendorID

GROUP BY V.Name, A.City, SP.Name, CR.Name
```

HAVING SUM(TotalDue) < $26000 -- HAVING clause predicate

ORDER BY SUM(TotalDue) DESC, Vendor;

Vendor	TotalPurchase	City	State	Country
Speed Corporation	$25,732.84	Anacortes	Washington	United States
Gardner Touring Cycles	$25,633.64	Altadena	California	United States
National Bike Association	$25,513.90	Sedro Woolley	Washington	United States
Australia Bike Retailer	$25,060.04	Bellingham	Washington	United States
WestAmerica Bicycle Co.	$25,060.04	Houston	Texas	United States
Ready Rentals	$23,635.06	Kirkland	Washington	United States
Morgan Bike	$23,146.99	Albany	New York	United

Accessori es				State s
Continent al Pro Cycles	$22,960.0 7	Long Beach	California	Unite d State s
American Bicycles and Wheels	$9,641.01	West Covina	California	Unite d State s
Litware, Inc.	$8,553.32	Santa Cruz	California	Unite d State s
Business Equipmen t Center	$8,497.80	Everett	Montana	Unite d State s
Bloomingt on Multisport	$8,243.95	West Covina	California	Unite d State s
Internatio nal	$8,061.10	Salt Lake City	Utah	Unite d State s
Wide World Importers	$8,025.60	Concord	California	Unite d State s
Midwest Sport, Inc.	$7,328.72	Detroit	Michigan	Unite d State s

Wood Fitness	$6,947.58	Philadelphia	Pennsylvania	United States
Metro Sport Equipment	$6,324.53	Lebanon	Oregon	United States
Burnett Road Warriors	$5,779.99	Corvallis	Oregon	United States
Lindell	$5,412.57	Lebanon	Oregon	United States
Consumer Cycles	$3,378.17	Torrance	California	United States
Northern Bike Travel	$2,048.42	Anacortes	Washington	United States

Chapter 2 SQL Data Types

In this chapter you will learn the role of data in a database model, how it is defined, its characteristics and the various types that the SQL software supports. There are general data types that are further categorized into different subtypes. It is advisable that you use defined data types to ensure the portability and comprehensibility of the database model.

Data Definition

Data is the stored information in a database that you can manipulate anytime that you want. If you can remember the calling card example in its database model is a collection of customers' names, contact numbers, company addresses, job titles and so on. When rules are provided on how to write and store data, then you need to have a clear understanding of the different *data types*. You need to take into consideration the length or space allocated by the database for every table column and what data values it should contain - whether it is just all letters or all numbers, combination or alphanumeric, graphical, date or time. By defining what data type is stored in each field during the design phase, data entry errors will be prevented. This is the *field definition* process, a form of validation that controls how incorrect data is to be entered into the database.

When a certain database field does not have any data items at all, then the value is unknown or what is called a *null value*. This is completely different from the numeric zero or the blank character value, since zeroes and blanks are still considered definite values. Check out the following scenarios when you might have a null value:

- Even if the data value could possibly exist, you don't know what it is yet.
- The value does not really exist yet.
- The value could be out of range.
- The field is not appropriate for a particular row.

SQL Data Types

These are the general types of SQL data types and their subtypes.

- *Numeric* – The value defined by this data type is either an exact or an approximate number.

1.   Exact Numeric

1.   *INTEGER* – This consists of positive and negative whole numbers without any decimal nor a fractional part. The INTEGER data value ranges from negative 2,147,483,648 to positive

2,147,483,647, with a maximum storage size of four bytes.

1) *SMALLINT* – This replaces integers when you want to save some storage space. However, its precision cannot be larger than that of an integer. Precision in computer programming is the maximum total of significant digits a certain number can have. The SMALLINT data value ranges from negative 32,768 to positive 32,767, with a maximum storage size of two bytes.

1) *BIGINT* – This is the reverse of SMALLINT, in which the minimum precision is the same or greater than that of an INTEGER. The BIGINT data value ranges from negative 9,223,372,036,854,775,808 to positive 9,223,372,036,854,775,807, with a maximum storage size of eight bytes.

Chapter 3   *NUMERIC (p, s)* – This data type contains an integer part and a fractional part that indicates the precision and scale of the data value. Scale is the number of digits reserved in the fractional part of the data value (located at the right side of the decimal point). In NUMERIC (p, s), *'p'* specifies the precision while *'s'* specifies the scale. For example, NUMERIC (6, 3) means that the number has a total of 6 significant digits with 3 digits following the decimal point.

Therefore, its absolute value will only be up to 999.999.

- *DECIMAL (p, s)* – This also has a fractional component where you can specify both the data value's precision and scale, but allows for greater precision. For example, DECIMAL (6, 3) can contain values up to 999.999 but the database will still accept values larger than 999.999 by rounding off the number. Let us say you entered the number 123.4564, the value that will be stored is 123.456. Thus, the precision given specifies the allocated storage size for this data type.

- **Approximate Numeric**
- *REAL (s)* – This is a single-precision, floating-point number where the decimal point can "float" within the said number. This gives a limitless precision and a scale of variable lengths for the data type's decimal value. For example, the values for п (pi) can include 3.1, 3.14 and 3.14159 (each value has its own precision). This data type's precision ranges from 1 up to 21, with a maximum storage size of four bytes.

1. *DOUBLE PRECISION (p, s)* – As what the name suggests, this is a double-precision, floating-point number with a storage capacity of twice the REAL data type. This data type is suitable when you

require more precise numbers, such as in most scientific field of disciplines. This data type's precision ranges from 22 up to 53 digits, with a maximum storage size of eight bytes.

1) *FLOAT (p, s)* – This data type lets you specify the value's precision and the computer decides whether it will be a single or a double-precision number. It will allow both the precision of REAL and DOUBLE PRECISION data types. Such features make it easier to move the database from one computer platform to another.

1)   *String* – Considered as the most commonly used data type, this stores alphanumeric information.

• *CHARACTER (n)* or *CHAR (n)* – Known as a fixed-length string or a constant character, this data type contains strings that have the same length (represented by *'n'*, which is the maximum number of characters allocated for the defined field). For example, setting the column's data type to CHAR (23) means the maximum length of the data to be stored in that field is 23 characters. If its length is less than 23, then the remaining spaces are filled with blanks by SQL. However, this becomes the downside of using fixed-length strings because storage space is totally wasted. On the other hand, if the length is not specified, then SQL assumes a length of just one character. The CHARACTER data type can have a maximum length of 254 characters.

1) *CHARACTER VARYING (n)* or *VARCHAR (n)* – This data type is for entries that have different lengths, but the remaining spaces will not be filled by spaces. This means that the exact number of characters entered will be stored in the database to avoid space wastage. The maximum length for this data type is 32,672 characters with no default value.

- *CHARACTER LARGE OBJECT (CLOB)* – This was introduced in SQL:1999 where the variable-length data type is used, which contains a Unicode, character-based information. Such data is too big to be stored as a CHARACTER type, just like large documents, and the maximum value is up to 2,147,483,647 characters long.

- ***Date and Time* – This data type handles information associated with dates and times.**
  - *DATE* – This provides a storage space for the date's year, month and day values (in that particular order). The value for the year is expressed in four digits (represented by values ranging from 0001

up to 9999), while the month and day values are both represented by any two digits. The format of this data type is: *'yyyy-mm-dd.'*

- *TIME* – This stores and displays time values using an hour-minute-second format (*"HH:MM:SS"*).

- *DATETIME* – This contains both date and time information displayed using the "YYYY-MM-DD HH:MM:SS" format. The range of this data type is from "1000-01-01 00:00:00" to "9999-12-31 23:59:59".

1) *TIMESTAMP* – Similar to the DATETIME data type, this ranges from "1970-01-01 00:00:01" UTC to "2038-01-19 03:14:07" UTC.

- *Boolean* – This data type is used for comparing information and based from the results they can return TRUE, FALSE, or NULL values. If all the conditions for a given query are met, then Boolean value returns TRUE. Otherwise, the value is either FALSE or NULL.

User-Defined Data Type

We will now discuss user-defined data types or simply UDT's. By the name itself, the user defines or specifies the data values based on the existing data types. This allows customization to meet other user requirements and maximize the available storage space. Moreover, programmers enjoy the flexibility they bring in developing database applications. UDT's make it possible when you need to store the same type of data in a column that will also be defined in several tables. The CREATE TYPE statement is used to define UDT's.

For example, if you need to use two different currencies for your database like the US dollar and the UK pound, you can create and define the following UDT's:

CREATE TYPE USDollar AS DECIMAL (9, 2) ;

CREATE TYPE UKPound AS DECIMAL (9, 2) ;

1) Data is the stored information in a database that a user can define and manipulate.

2) There are different general SQL data types, namely numeric, string, date and time, and Boolean.

3) If you want to define more specific data types when designing your database model, you can use the different subtypes under each general SQL data type.

4) UDT's or user-defined data types are customized and created by the user based on the existing data types, which gives flexibility in developing various database applications.

In the next chapter you will learn the common SQL commands that are used to create, manipulate and retrieve data from a database, in an efficient and effective way.

Chapter 4 Cursors: Read Only, Forward Only, Fast Forward, Static, Scroll, Dynamic, Optimistic

Cursors are database objects that are used to iterate over a set of rows and generally perform some additional logical operations or others on each row of fetched data. The process of cursor operation entails following tasks:

- *Declare the variables to be used*
- *Define the Cursor and type of cursor*
- *Populate Cursor with values using SELECT*
- *Open Cursor that was declared & populated above*
  - Fetch the values from Cursor in to declared variables
- *While loop to fetch next row and loop till no longer rows exist*
  - Perform any data processing on that row inside while loop
- *Close Cursor to gracefully un-lock tables in any*
- *Remove Cursor from memory*

However, Cursors are generally not recommended due to row-by-row fetching and processing of data, consumption of memory (due to allocation of temporary table and filling it with the result set) and sometimes locking tables in unpredictable ways. Thus, alternate approaches like using *while* loop needs to be considered before using cursors.

LOCAL/GLOBAL CURSOR

This cursor specifies the scope and whether this scope allows locally to a stored procedure or trigger or even a batch OR if the scope of the cursor is applicable globally for the connection. Cursor is valid only within the scope defined.

FORWARD_ONLY CURSOR

FORWARD_ONLY Cursor specifies that rows can only be scrolled from first to the end row. Thus, this precludes moving to *prior* or *last* row and *fetch next* is only option available. Below is an example of *FORWARD_ONLY Cursor*:

```
--
==================================
==============
-- Author:          Neal Gupta
-- Create date: 12/01/2013
-- Description: Create a Cursor for displaying customer info
```

```
--
================================
==============
DECLARE
          @CustomerID INT
          ,@FirstName VARCHAR(50)
    ,@LastName VARCHAR(50)
          ,@City VARCHAR(50)
          ,@State VARCHAR(10)
          ,@ZipCode VARCHAR(10)
-- Create a Cursor
DECLARE         curTblCustomer         CURSOR
FORWARD  ONLY
FOR
SELECT
          CustomerID, FirstName, LastName, City,
[State], ZipCode
FROM [IMS].[dbo].[TblCustomer]
ORDER BY CustomerID ASC;
-- Open the Cursor
OPEN curTblCustomer
-- Get the first Customer
```

```sql
FETCH NEXT FROM curTblCustomer INTO
@CustomerID, @FirstName, @LastName, @City,
@State,@ZipCode

PRINT 'Customer Details:'

-- Loop thru all the customers

WHILE @@FETCH_STATUS = 0
        BEGIN
            -- Display customer details

        PRINT        CAST(@CustomerID        AS
        VARCHAR(50)) + ' ' + @FirstName + ' ' +
        @LastName + ' '+ @City + ' '+ @State + '
        '+ @ZipCode
            -- Get the next customer

        FETCH NEXT FROM curTblCustomer INTO
        @CustomerID, @FirstName, @LastName,
        @City, @State, @ZipCode
END

-- Close Cursor

CLOSE curTblCustomer

-- Remove Cursor from memory of temp database

DEALLOCATE curTblCustomer
```

Cursor by default is FORWARD_ONLY, if *STATIC,
KEYSET* or *DYNAMIC* options are not mentioned and
cursor works as a *DYNAMIC* one if these 3 keywords
are not specified.

READ_ONLY CURSOR

This cursor is similar to above *FORWARD_ONLY* cursor, except that updates on the current fetched row cannot be performed.

FAST_FORWARD CURSOR

This cursor is really a combination of *FAST_FORWARD* (#1) and *READ_ONLY* (#2) along with performance optimizations. Since, it is a *fast forward* cursor, it precludes scrolling to prior or last row and being *read only* cursor also, prevents update of current fetched row. However, due to these 2 restrictions, they help SQL server to optimize the overall cursor performance.

```
--
===============================================
-- Description: Create a FAST_FORWARD Cursor
===============================================
DECLARE
          @CustomerID INT
          ,@FirstName VARCHAR(50)
       ,@LastName VARCHAR(50)
          ,@City VARCHAR(50)
          ,@State VARCHAR(10)
```

```
              ,@ZipCode VARCHAR(10)

-- Create a Cursor

DECLARE curTblCustomer CURSOR FAST_FORWARD

FOR

SELECT

          CustomerID

    ,FirstName
    ,LastName
    ,City
    ,[State]
    ,ZipCode
FROM

    [IMS].[dbo].[TblCustomer]
ORDER BY

    CustomerID ASC;
-- Open the Cursor

OPEN curTblCustomer

-- Get the first Customer

FETCH   NEXT   FROM   curTblCustomer   INTO
@CustomerID,  @FirstName,  @LastName,  @City,
@State, @ZipCode

PRINT 'Customer Details:'

-- Loop thru all the customers

WHILE @@FETCH_STATUS = 0
```

```
        BEGIN
            -- Display customer details
    PRINT          CAST(@CustomerID        AS
    VARCHAR(50)) + ' ' + @FirstName + ' ' +
    @LastName + ' '+ @City + ' '+ @State + '
    '+ @ZipCode
            -- Get the next customer
    FETCH NEXT FROM curTblCustomer INTO
    @CustomerID, @FirstName, @LastName,
    @City, @State, @ZipCode
END

-- Close Cursor

CLOSE curTblCustomer

-- Remove Cursor from memory of temp database

DEALLOCATE curTblCustomer
```

STATIC CURSOR

If a cursor is specified as *STATIC*, SQL server takes a snapshot of the data and places into temporary table in *tempdb* database. So, when the cursor fetches next row, data comes from this temporary table and therefore, if something is modified in the original table, it is not reflected in the temporary table. This makes the performance of cursor faster as compared to dynamic cursor (explained below) since next row of data is already pre-fetched in temp database.

DYNAMIC CURSOR

As the name suggests, when the cursor is scrolling to next row, data for that row is dynamically brought from the original table, and if there was any change, it is reflected in the data fetched as well.

SCROLL CURSOR

This cursor allows scrolling of rows: *FIRST, LAST, PRIOR, NEXT* and if a cursor is not specified as SCROLL, it can only perform *FETCH* next row. If the cursor is *FAST_FORWARD, SCROLL* option cannot be used.

OPTIMISTIC/SCROLL_LOCKS CURSOR

Below is a cursor declaration using some of the above options: *LOCAL, FORWARD_ONLY, STATIC and READ_ONLY*:

DECLARE curTblCustomerOp1 CURSOR

   LOCAL

   FORWARD_ONLY

   STATIC

   READ_ONLY

FOR

-- Rest of SQL remains same as used in FORWARD_ONLY Cursor

Another cursor declaration could use following options: *GLOBAL, SCROLL, DYNAMIC, OPTIMISTIC:*

DECLARE curTblCustomerOp2 CURSOR

    GLOBAL   -- OR USE LOCAL

    SCROLL   -- OR USE FORWARD_ONLY

    DYNAMIC   --   OR   USE FAST_FORWARD/STATIC/KEYSET

    OPTIMISTIC   --   OR   USE READ_ONLY/SCROLL_LOCKS

FOR

-- Rest of SQL remains same as used in FORWARD_ONLY Cursor

NESTED CURSOR

As the name suggest, cursors can be nested, meaning one cursor can have another inner cursor and so on. In below example we will use one nested cursor.

--
==

-- Description: Create a Nested Cursor for displaying Orders

-- and products ordered

```sql
--
================================
==============

DECLARE
            @OrderID INT
            ,@ProductID INT
            ,@OrderQty INT
            ,@OrderDate DATETIME
            ,@Name VARCHAR(50)
            ,@Manufacturer VARCHAR(50)
            ,@Price DECIMAL(9,2)
PRINT '***** Orders Details *****'
--- First, declare OUTER Cursor
DECLARE curTblOrder CURSOR
            LOCAL
    FORWARD ONLY
    STATIC
            READ ONLY
    TYPE WARNING
FOR
            SELECT
                    OrderID
```

```sql
                ,ProductID

                ,OrderQty

                ,OrderDate

        FROM

                [IMS].[dbo].[TblOrder]

        ORDER BY

                OrderID

-- Open OUTER Cursor

OPEN curTblOrder

-- Fetch data from cursor and populate into variables

FETCH NEXT FROM curTblOrder INTO @OrderID, @ProductID, @OrderQty, @OrderDate

WHILE @@FETCH_STATUS = 0

BEGIN

        PRINT '*** Order: ' + ' ' + CAST(@OrderID AS VARCHAR(10))

    -- Now, declare INNER Cursor

    DECLARE curTblProduct CURSOR

        FOR

                SELECT Name, Manufacturer, Price
```

```sql
                    FROM [IMS].[dbo].[TblProduct]
P

                        WHERE    P.ProductID    =
@ProductID


        -- Open INNER Cursor
   OPEN curTblProduct

   FETCH NEXT FROM curTblProduct INTO @Name,
@Manufacturer, @Price
            -- Loop for INNER Cursor
        WHILE @@FETCH_STATUS = 0
   BEGIN
PRINT 'Product: ' + @Name + ' ' + @Manufacturer
+ ' ' + CAST(@Price AS VARCHAR(15))

                FETCH NEXT FROM curTblProduct
INTO @Name, @Manufacturer, @Price
        END
        -- Close INNER Cursor first and deallocate
it from temp database
   CLOSE curTblProduct

   DEALLOCATE curTblProduct

   -- Fetch next Order
```

FETCH NEXT FROM **curTblOrder** INTO **@OrderID**, **@ProductID**, **@OrderQty**, @OrderDate

END

-- Finally, close OUTER Cursor and deallocate it from temp database

CLOSE curTblOrder

DEALLOCATE curTblOrder

FOR UPDATE CURSOR

This cursor allows updating the column values in the fetched row for the specified columns only, however, if the columns are not specified, then, all the columns can be updated for the row under consideration using *WHERE CURRENT OF* clause.

ALTERNATIVE APPROACH

Note that in above examples, we used cursors to demonstrate the functionality of different types of cursor, however, we could have used alternative approach, like using *WHILE* loop and *counter* approach to perform similar task, as was done in #2 above, as below:

```
--
================================
==============
-- Description: Alternative Approach
```

```sql
-- using WHILE loop and Counter Method
--
================================
==============
    DECLARE @Customers TABLE
     RowID INT IDENTITY(1,1) PRIMARY KEY
     ,CustomerID INT
     ,FirstName VARCHAR(50)
     ,LastName VARCHAR(50)
     ,City VARCHAR(50)
     ,[State] VARCHAR(25)
     ,ZipCode VARCHAR(10)
    DECLARE
         @StartCount INT = 1          -- First
Row Count
         ,@EndCount  INT                    --
Total Row Counts
             ,@CustomerID INT
             ,@FirstName VARCHAR(50)
             ,@LastName VARCHAR(50)
             ,@City VARCHAR(50)
             ,@State VARCHAR(50)
             ,@ZipCode VARCHAR(10)
```

```sql
-- Bulk Insert all the customers into temp table: @Customers

INSERT INTO @Customers (CustomerID,FirstName,LastName,City,[State],Zip Code)

SELECT
        CustomerID
        ,FirstName
        ,LastName
        ,City
        ,[State]
        ,ZipCode
FROM
        [IMS].[dbo].[TblCustomer] WITH (NOLOCK)

-- EndCount is set to total of all rows fetched in above SELECT

SELECT @EndCount = @@ROWCOUNT

-- Loop thru all the rows

WHILE @StartCount <= @EndCount
BEGIN
        SELECT
                @CustomerID = CustomerID
```

```sql
        ,@FirstName = FirstName
        ,@LastName = LastName
        ,@City = City
        ,@State = [State]
        ,@ZipCode = ZipCode
    FROM @Customers
    WHERE
        RowID = @StartCount


PRINT 'Fetched Row#: ' + CAST(@StartCount AS
VARCHAR(5)) + ' from TblCustomer table. Details
below: '
            PRINT 'CustomerID = '+
CAST(@CustomerID AS VARCHAR(5)) + '
        FirstName = ' + @FirstName + '
LastName = ' + @LastName + ' City
            = ' + @City + ' State = ' +
@State + ' ZipCode = ' + @ZipCode
        SELECT @StartCount += 1
END
```

Chapter 5 Preparation

To successfully connect to and work with a SQL Server Database from your Windows PC (desktop or notebook), there are several things that must be properly setup or configured. None of these are very complex, but failure to address these items can and will result in either problems, warnings and/or errors. So while this chapter may be brief, the basic concepts (and their mental images) are nonetheless very critical for your success. So it would be wise to read and learn this chapter's material well.

Database Architecture

The SQL Server database itself will most often reside upon a server somewhere within your organization. While you can both run and access the SQL Server database on most PC's these days, the raw performance, tight security and high availability requirements alone generally require a secure, centrally managed database server.

Database Architecture

The critical item of note is that both the client and the server need some supporting SQL Server network library files in order for communication between your application and the database to occur. Because it's not necessary to know anything about

TDS to connect to a SQL Server database, we won't delve any further into the specifics about it.

What is important is you must have those network library files on your PC for database connections to function properly. Since Windows 2000, all versions of Windows have at least a basic set of these network library files already pre-installed. SQL Server 2005 introduced a new set of network files called the SQL Server Native Client which provides additional functionality based on new features that was added to that version of SQL Server. The features are not essential to retrieve data from a SQL Server database but center around security and management functionality such as the ability to handle passwords similar to the way Windows does. However, if you don't use these additional features, chances are you already have everything you need to connect to the SQL Server database.

Database Versions

The SQL Server database, like most software, has different versions – such as SQL Server 2000, 2005, 2008, and 2008 R2. These are simply the marketing names for the initial or base releases. In addition there are numerous patches available, usually called service packs or cumulative updates. If you're experiencing an issue with something not working the way you'd expect it to, you might check with your system administrator or database administrator to see if one of these is needed. But typically they are only required if you installed specific client software from the SQL Server CDs/DVDs.

Connecting

Thus far we've primarily covered terminology and that is a prerequisite for successfully working with your SQL Server databases. Now it's time to perform your very first SQL Server database task – connecting to your database. That may seem like an anticlimactic task but it's the first step in making use of the data within those databases.

Think of creating the database connection like making a phone call. If you don't have the proper equipment, a service plan, the number of whom you're calling and knowledge of how to dial that number, then you cannot initiate a phone call and thus cannot hold a meaningful conversation. The same is true for databases. You must successfully connect before you can retrieve, insert or update your data.

Connecting Via ODBC

A lot of applications connect to SQL Server using a method called ODBC. Either the application will present an interface where you can create your connection or it will ask you for an existing ODBC connection. Chances are that if it presents an interface, the steps will be similar to when you create your own ODBC connection. In fact, a lot of times applications will simply re-use Windows' own tool for managing these connections. So let's look at how to do that.

Control Panel icon

You'll want to click on it and that will bring up the Control Panel. If you're in Classic View, you should see an icon for Administrative Tools. If you're in Category View you'll have to double-click on the Performance and Maintenance icon first. Once you see the Administrative Tools icon, double-click on it and you should have a new list of options. What you're looking for is the icon for Data Sources (ODBC). Double-click on it and it will bring up the tool ODBC Administrator where you'll be able to configure a new ODBC connection.

There are two types of data sources called data set names (i.e. DSN): user and system. User ones can only be seen and used by the current Windows user, whereas system ones can be seen and used by any Windows user on that same PC.

ODBC Admin Main Screen

Here we have a good number of choices, but usually you'll just want the one that says SQL Server. In this example, the full SQL Server tools are installed for several versions of SQL Server, which is why you also see choices for SQL Server Native Client. You likely won't have the SQL Server Native Client choices unless you need them. Simply select SQL Server and click Finish.

SQL Server Data Source

In the event that you'll one day need to connect to a different database server (Oracle, DB2, etc.) generally speaking you will have the most reliable results and fastest performance using the ODBC driver from the database vendor and it likely will be named so you easily recognize it.

Choose the Name and SQL Server

You'll then need to choose how you connect to the SQL Server in the sense of how does SQL Server know who you are. Most of the time, you'll connect using the user account you logged on to Windows with. If you need a special SQL Server login, your system or database administrator should provide it ahead of time, along with the appropriate password.

In either case, make the appropriate selections for the next screen,

Tell SQL Server Who You Are

Next, you'll need to specify any other options for the connection. Here you'll want to check the checkbox to change the default database and then choose the right one from the drop down list. If you should get an error here, it means either the SQL Server you specified in the previous screen is not available, or you mistyped its name, or you don't have permission to connect. If that's the case, go back to the previous screen, check the name of the SQL Server, and if you believe it's right, follow up with your system or database administrator. It could be down or there could be another reason as to why you can't connect to it.

Specify the Database

This is the database I know contains the sales information I want to access. You'll need to know both the server and the database name to get at the data stored on the SQL Server.

Click the Next button to go to the last configuration screen, where you likely won't need to make any changes, then click Finish to create your ODBC connection. You should be presented with a screen like in - be sure to test your connection to make sure everything is fine before clicking OK.

Review Setup

Conclusion

In this chapter we reviewed the basic concepts and processes you need to understand and perform in order to begin successfully working with your SQL Server databases. We also reviewed covered the prerequisite knowledge to tackle the first and most critical database task – connecting. Much like a phone call – we entered the information necessary to dial in to the database and then placed the call.

Chapter 6 Filters

WHERE Clause

WHERE is the most widely used clause. It helps retrieve exactly what you require. The following example table displays the STUDENT STRENGTH in various Engineering courses in a college:

ENGINEERING_STUDENTS

ENGG_ID	ENGG_NAME	STUDENT_STRENGTH
1	Electronics	150
2	Software	250
3	Genetic	75
4	Mechanical	150
5	Biomedical	72
6	Instrumentation	80
7	Chemical	75
8	Civil	60

9	Electronics & Com	250
10	Electrical	60

Now, if you want to know how many courses have over 200 in STUDENT STRENGTH, then you can simplify your search by passing on a simple statement:

SELECT ENGG_NAME, STUDENT_STRENGTH

FROM ENGINEERING_STUDENTS

WHERE STUDENT_STRENGTH > 200;

ENGG_NAME	STUDENT_STRENGTH
Software	250
Electronics & Com	250

HAVING Clause

HAVING is another clause used as a filter in SQL. At this point, it is important to understand the difference between the WHERE and HAVING clauses. WHERE specifies a condition, and only that set of data that passes the condition will be fetched and displayed in the result set. HAVING clause is used to filter grouped or summarized data. If a SELECT query has both WHERE and HAVING clauses, then when WHERE is used to filter rows, the result is aggregated so the HAVING clause can be applied. You will get a better understanding when you see an example.

For an explanation, another table by the name of Dept_Data has been created, and it is defined as follows:

Field	Type	Null	Key	Default	Extra
Dept_ ID	Bigint (20)	NO	PRI	NULL	auto_ increment
HOD	Varchar (35)	NO			
NO_ OF_ Prof	Varchar (35)	YES		NULL	
ENGG_ ID	Smallint (6)	YES	MUL	NULL	

Now, let's have a look at the data available in this table:

Where Dept_ID is set to 100.

Dept_ID	HOD	NO_OF_Prof	ENGG_ID
100	Miley Andrews	7	1
101	Alex Dawson	6	2
102	Victoria Fox	7	3
103	Anne Joseph	5	4
104	Sophia Williams	8	5
105	Olive Brown	4	6
106	Joshua Taylor	6	7
107	Ethan Thomas	5	8

| 108 | Michael Anderson | 8 | 9 |
| 109 | Martin Jones | 5 | 10 |

There are a few simple differences between the WHERE and HAVING clauses. The WHERE clause can be used with SELECT, UPDATE, and DELETE clauses, but the HAVING clause does not enjoy that privilege; it is only used in the SELECT query. The WHERE clause can be used for individual rows, but HAVING is applied on grouped data. If the WHERE and HAVING clauses are used together, then the WHERE clause will be used before the GROUP BY clause, and the HAVING clause will be used after the GROUP BY clause. Whenever WHERE and HAVING clauses are used together in a query, the WHERE clause is applied first on every row to filter the results and ensure a group is created. After that, you will apply the HAVING clause on that group.

Now, based on our previous tables, let's see which departments have more than 5 professors:

SELECT * FROM Dept_Data WHERE NO_OF_Prof > 5;

Look at the WHERE clause here. It will check each and every row to see which record has NO_OF_Prof > 5.

Dept_ID	HOD	NO_OF_Prof	ENGG_ID
100	Miley Andrews	7	1
101	Alex Dawson	6	2
102	Victoria Fox	7	3
104	Sophia Williams	8	5
106	Joshua Taylor	6	7
108	Michael Anderson	8	9

Now, let's find the names of the Engineering courses for the above data:

SELECT e. ENGG_NAME, e.STUDENT_STRENGTH,

d.HOD,d.NO_OF_Prof,d.Dept_ID

FROM ENGINEERING_STUDENTS e, Dept_Data d

WHERE d.NO_OF_Prof > 5

AND e.ENGG_ID = d.ENGG_ID;

The result set will be as follows:

ENGG_NAME	STUDENT_STRENGTH	HOD	NO_OF_Prof	Dept_ID
Electronics	150	Miley Andrews	7	100
Software	250	Alex Dawson	6	101
Genetic	75	Victoria Fox	7	102
Biomedical	72	Sophia Williams	8	104
Chemical	75	Joshua Taylor	6	106
Electronics & Com	250	Michael Anderson	8	108

Next, we GROUP the data as shown below:

SELECT e.ENGG_NAME, d.HOD,d.NO_OF_Prof,d.Dept_ID

FROM ENGINEERING_STUDENTS e, Dept_Data d

WHERE d.NO_OF_Prof > 5 AND e.ENGG_ID = d.ENGG_ID

GROUP BY ENGG_NAME;

ENGG_NAME	STUDENT_STRENGTH	HOD	NO_OF_Prof	Dept_ID
Biomedical	72	Sophia Williams	8	104
Chemical	75	Joshua Taylor	6	106
Electronics	150	Miley Andrews	7	100
Electronics & Com	250	Michael Anderson	8	108

Genetic	75	Victoria Fox	7	102
Software	250	Alex Dawson	6	101

Let's see which departments from this group have more than 100 students:

SELECT e. ENGG_NAME, e.STUDENT_STRENGTH,

d.HOD,d.NO_OF_Prof,d.Dept_ID

FROM ENGINEERING_STUDENTS e, Dept_Data d

WHERE d.NO_OF_Prof > 5 AND e.ENGG_ID = d.ENGG_ID
GROUP BY e.ENGG_NAME HAVING e.STUDENT_STRENGTH > 100;

ENGG_NAME	STUDENT_STRENGTH	HOD	NO_OF_Prof	Dept_ID
Electronics	150	Miley Andrews	7	100

Electronics & Com	250	Michael Anderson	8	108
Software	250	Alex Dawson	6	101

Evaluating a Condition

A WHERE clause can evaluate more than one condition where every condition is separated by the AND operator. Let's take a look at the example below:

SELECT e. ENGG_NAME, e.STUDENT_STRENGTH,

d.HOD,d.NO_OF_Prof,d.Dept_ID

FROM ENGINEERING_STUDENTS e, Dept_Data d

WHERE d.NO_OF_Prof > 5 AND

e.ENGG_ID = d.ENGG_ID AND

100 < e.STUDENT_STRENGTH < 250;

ENGG_NAME	STUDENT_STRENGTH	HOD	NO_OF_Prof	Dept_ID
Electronics	150	Miley Andrews	7	100
Software	250	Alex Dawson	6	101
Genetic	75	Victoria Fox	7	102
Biomedical	72	Sophia Williams	8	104
Chemical	75	Joshua Taylor	6	106
Electronics & Com	250	Michael Anderson	8	108

There is one thing you must understand with the WHERE clause. It is only when all conditions become true for a row that it is included in the result set. If even one condition turns out to be false, the row will not be included in the result set.

The result set will be different if you replace any or all AND operators in the above statement with the OR operator. Say you need to find out which department has either fewer than 100 students OR fewer than 5 professors. Have a look at the following statement:

SELECT e. ENGG_NAME,e.STUDENT_STRENGTH,

d.HOD,d.NO_OF_Prof,d.Dept_ID,e.ENGG_ID

FROM ENGINEERING_STUDENTS e, Dept_Data d

WHERE e.ENGG_ID = d.ENGG_ID AND

(e.STUDENT_STRENGTH < 100 OR d.NO_OF_Prof < 5);

ENGG_NAME	STUDENT_STRENGTH	HOD	NO_OF_Prof	Dept_ID
Genetic	75	Victoria Fox	7	102

Biomedical	72	Sophia Williams	8	104
Instrumentation	80	Olive Brown	4	105
Chemical	75	Joshua Taylor	6	106
Civil	60	Ethan Thomas	5	107
Electrical	60	Martin Jones	5	109

In the above statement, notice how the parentheses are placed. You should clearly define how the AND operator exists between two conditions, and how the OR operator exists between two conditions. You will learn more about the usage of parentheses in the upcoming section. For now, please understand how the outcome of the AND/OR operators are evaluated.

AND Operator

Condition	Outcome
Where True AND True	True
Where False AND True	False
Where True AND False	False
Where False AND False	False

OR Operator

Condition	Outcome
Where True OR True	True
Where False OR True	True
Where True OR False	True
Where False OR False	False

Usage of Parentheses

In the last example, we had three conditions, and we put one condition in parentheses. If the parentheses are missing, the results will be wrong and confusing. For a change, let's try and see what happens if this occurs:

SELECT e.ENGG_NAME,e.STUDENT_STRENGTH,

d.HOD,d.NO_OF_Prof,d.Dept_ID,e.ENGG_ID

FROM ENGINEERING_STUDENTS e, DEPT_DATA d

WHERE e.ENGG_ID = d.ENGG_ID AND

e.STUDENT_STRENGTH < 100 OR d.NO_OF_Prof < 5;

ENGG_ NAME	STUDE NT_ STREN GTH	HOD	NO _ OF _ Pr of	Dept_ ID	ENGG _ID
Genetic	75	Victor ia Fox	7	102	3
Biomedical	72	Sophi a Willia ms	8	104	5

Electronics	150	Olive Brown	4	105	1
Software	250	Olive Brown	4	105	2
Genetic	75	Olive Brown	4	105	3
Mechanical	150	Olive Brown	4	105	4
Biomedical	72	Olive Brown	4	105	5
Instrumentation	80	Olive Brown	4	105	6
Chemical	75	Olive Brown	4	105	7

Civil	60	Olive Brown	4	105	8
Electronics & Com	250	Olive Brown	4	105	9
Electrical	60	Olive Brown	4	105	10
Chemical	75	Joshua Taylor	6	106	7
Civil	60	Ethan Thomas	5	107	8
Electrical	60	Martin Jones	5	109	10

One look at the table above and you know the results are all wrong and misleading. The reason is that the instructions are not clear to the data server. Now, think about what we want to accomplish; we want to know which department has fewer than 100 students OR fewer than 5 professors. Now, witness the magic of the parentheses. The parentheses convert three conditions to two, well-defined conditions.

WHERE e.ENGG_ID = d.ENGG_ID AND

(e.STUDENT_STRENGTH < 100 OR d.NO_OF_Prof < 5);

This follows the following format: Condition1 AND (Condition2 OR Condition3).

Now, this is how the condition will be calculated:

Cond1	Cond2	Cond3	Cond2 OR Cond3	Cond1 AND (Cond2 OR Cond3)
T	T	T	T	T
T	T	F	T	T
T	F	T	T	T
T	F	F	F	F

F	T	T	T	F
F	T	F	T	F
F	F	T	T	F
F	F	F	F	F

By putting e.STUDENT_STRENGTH < 100 OR d.NO_OF_Prof < 5 into parentheses, we convert it into one condition, and the first condition will consider the output of the parentheses for the final result. Out of eight possible conditions from the table above, there are only three scenarios where the final condition is True.

The NOT Operator

To understand the usage of the NOT operator, let's replace AND with AND NOT and find out what output we receive:

SELECT e. ENGG_NAME,e.STUDENT_STRENGTH,

d.HOD,d.NO_OF_Prof,d.Dept_ID,e.ENGG_ID

FROM ENGINEERING_STUDENTS e, Dept_Data d

WHERE e.ENGG_ID = d.ENGG_ID AND NOT

(e.STUDENT_STRENGTH < 100 OR d.NO_OF_Prof < 5);

ENGG_ NAME	STUDENT _ STRENGT H	HOD	NO _ OF_ Prof	Dept _ ID	ENGG _ ID
Electronic s	150	Miley Andrews	7	100	1
Software	250	Alex Dawson	6	101	2
Mechanic al	150	Anne Joseph	5	103	4
Electronic s & Com	250	Michael Anderso n	8	108	9

Remember that our desired results find which department has fewer than 100 students or fewer than 5 professors. After applying the NOT operator before the parentheses, our results look for either more than 5 professors, or more than 100 students.

Is it possible to obtain the same results while using the NOT statement? Yes! Just replace '>' with '<' and replace OR with AND.

SELECT e.ENGG_NAME,e.STUDENT_STRENGTH,

d.HOD,d.NO_OF_Prof,d.Dept_ID,e.ENGG_ID

FROM ENGINEERING_STUDENTS e, Dept_Data d

WHERE e.ENGG_ID = d.ENGG_ID AND NOT

(e.STUDENT_STRENGTH ≥ 100 AND d.NO_OF_Prof ≥ 5);

ENGG_NAME	STUDENT_STRENGTH	HOD	NO_OF_Prof	Dept_ID	ENGG_ID
Genetic	75	Victoria Fox	7	102	3
Biomedical	72	Sophia Williams	8	104	5

Instrumentation	80	Olive Brown	4	105	6
Chemical	75	Joshua Taylor	6	106	7
Civil	60	Ethan Thomas	5	107	8
Electrical	60	Martin Jones	5	109	10

Here is the output for applying AND NOT:

Cond1	Cond2	Cond3	Cond2 AND Cond3	Cond1 AND NOT (Cond2 AND Cond3)
T	T	T	T	F
T	T	F	F	T
T	F	T	F	T
T	F	F	F	T

F	T	T	T	T
F	T	F	F	T
F	F	T	F	T
F	F	F	F	T

However, use the NOT operator only when required. It can aid in the legibility of the statement, but if you use NOT when it can be avoided, it could unnecessarily complicate things for the developer.

Sequences

A sequence refers to a set of numbers that has been generated in a specified order on demand. These are popular in databases. The reason behind this is that sequences provide an easy way to have a unique value for each row in a specified column. This section explains the use of sequences in SQL.

AUTO_INCREMENT Column

This provides you with the easiest way of creating a sequence in MySQL. You only have to define the column as auto_increment and leave MySQL to take care of the rest. To show how to use this property, we will create a simple table and insert some records into the table.

The following command will help us create the table:

```
CREATE TABLE colleagues

(

    id INT UNSIGNED NOT NULL AUTO_INCREMENT,

    PRIMARY KEY (id),

    name VARCHAR(20) NOT NULL,

    home_city VARCHAR(20) NOT NULL
);
```

The command should create the table successfully, as shown below:

```
mysql> create database tuw
    -> ;
Query OK, 1 row affected (0.05 sec)

mysql> use tuw;
Database changed
mysql> CREATE TABLE colleagues
    ->    (
    ->    id INT UNSIGNED NOT NULL AUTO_INCREMENT,
    ->    PRIMARY KEY (id),
    ->    name VARCHAR(20) NOT NULL,
    ->    home_city VARCHAR(20) NOT NULL
    -> );
Query OK, 0 rows affected (0.30 sec)

mysql>
```

We have created a table named colleagues. This table has 3 columns: id, name, and home_city. The first column is an integer data type while the rest are varchars (variable characters). We have added the auto_increment property to the id column, so the column values will be incremented automatically. When entering data into the table, we don't need to specify the value of this column. It will start at 1 by default then increment the values automatically for each record you insert into the table.

Let us now insert some records into the table:

INSERT INTO colleagues

VALUES (NULL, "John", "New Delhi");

INSERT INTO colleagues

VALUES (NULL, "Joel", "New Jersey");

INSERT INTO colleagues

VALUES (NULL, "Britney", "New York");

INSERT INTO colleagues

VALUES (NULL, "Biggy", "Washington");

The commands should run successfully, as shown below:

Now, we can run the select statement against the table and see its contents:

```
mysql> select * from colleagues;
+----+---------+-------------+
| id | name    | home_city   |
+----+---------+-------------+
|  1 | John    | New Delhi   |
|  2 | Joel    | New Jersey  |
|  3 | Britney | New York    |
|  4 | Biggy   | Washington  |
+----+---------+-------------+
4 rows in set (0.01 sec)

mysql>
```

We see that the id column has also been populated with values starting from 1. Each time you enter a record, the value of this column is increased by 1. We have successfully created a sequence.

Renumbering a Sequence

You notice that when you delete a record from a sequence such as the one we have created above, the records will not be renumbered. You may not be impressed by this kind of numbering. However, it is possible for you to re-sequence the records. This only involves a single trick, but make sure to check whether the table has a join with another table or not.

If you find you have to re-sequence your records, the best way to do it is by dropping the column and then adding it. Here, we'll show how to drop the id column of the colleagues table.

The table is as follows for now:

```
mysql> select * from colleagues;
+----+---------+------------+
| id | name    | home_city  |
+----+---------+------------+
|  1 | John    | New Delhi  |
|  2 | Joel    | New Jersey |
|  3 | Britney | New York   |
|  4 | Biggy   | Washington |
+----+---------+------------+
4 rows in set (0.01 sec)

mysql>
```

Let us drop the id column by running the following command:

ALTER TABLE colleagues DROP id;

146

```
mysql> ALTER TABLE colleagues DROP id;
Query OK, 4 rows affected (0.40 sec)
Records: 4  Duplicates: 0  Warnings: 0

mysql>
```

To confirm whether the deletion has taken place, let's take a look at the table data:

```
mysql> select * from colleagues;
+---------+------------+
| name    | home_city  |
+---------+------------+
| John    | New Delhi  |
| Joel    | New Jersey |
| Britney | New York   |
| Biggy   | Washington |
+---------+------------+
4 rows in set (0.00 sec)

mysql>
```

The deletion was successful. We combined the ALTER TABLE and the DROP commands for the deletion of the column. Now, let us re-add the column to the table:

ALTER TABLE colleagues

ADD id INT UNSIGNED NOT NULL AUTO_INCREMENT FIRST,

ADD PRIMARY KEY (id);

147

The command should run as follows:

```
mysql> ALTER TABLE colleagues
    ->      ADD id INT UNSIGNED NOT NULL AUTO_INCREMENT FIRST,
    ->      ADD PRIMARY KEY (id);
Query OK, 0 rows affected (0.76 sec)
Records: 0  Duplicates: 0  Warnings: 0
```

We started with the ALTER TABLE command to specify the name of the table we need to change. The ADD command has then been used to add the column and set it as the primary key for the table. We have also used the auto_increment property in the column definition. We can now query the table to see what has happened:

```
mysql> ALTER TABLE colleagues
    ->      ADD id INT UNSIGNED NOT NULL AUTO_INCREMENT FIRST,
    ->      ADD PRIMARY KEY (id);
Query OK, 0 rows affected (0.76 sec)
Records: 0  Duplicates: 0  Warnings: 0

mysql> select * from colleagues;
+----+---------+------------+
| id | name    | home_city  |
+----+---------+------------+
|  1 | John    | New Delhi  |
|  2 | Joel    | New Jersey |
|  3 | Britney | New York   |
|  4 | Biggy   | Washington |
+----+---------+------------+
4 rows in set (0.00 sec)

mysql>
```

The id column was added successfully. The sequence has also been numbered correctly.

MySQL starts the sequence at index 1 by default. However, it is possible for you to customize this when you are creating the table. You can set the limit or amount of the increment each time a record is created. Like in the table named colleagues, we can alter the table for the auto_increment to be done at intervals of 2. This is achieved through the code below:

ALTER TABLE colleagues AUTO_INCREMENT = 2;

The command should run successfully, as shown below:

```
mysql> ALTER TABLE colleagues AUTO_INCREMENT = 2;
Query OK, 0 rows affected (0.06 sec)
Records: 0  Duplicates: 0  Warnings: 0

mysql>
```

We can specify where the auto_increment will start at the time of the creation of the table. The following example shows this:

CREATE TABLE colleagues2

(

id INT UNSIGNED NOT NULL AUTO_INCREMENT = 10,

PRIMARY KEY (id),

name VARCHAR(20) NOT NULL,

home_city VARCHAR(20) NOT NULL

);

From the above instance, we set the auto_increment property on the id column, and the initial value for the column will be 10.

Chapter 7 14-SQL Subqueries

A sub-query refers to a query embedded inside another query, and this is done in the *WHERE* clause. It is also referred to as an Inner query or Nested query.

We use a sub-query to return the data that will be used in our main query and as a condition for restricting the data we are to retrieve. We can add sub-queries to *SELECT, UPDATE, INSERT,* and DELETE statements and combine them with operators like =, <, >, <=, >=, *IN, BETWEEN* and many others.

The following are the rules that govern the use of sub-queries:

·   A sub-query must be added within parenthesis.

·   A sub-query should return only one column, meaning that the SELECT * cannot be used within a sub-query unless where the table has only a single column. If your goal is to perform row comparison, you can create a sub-query that will return multiple columns.

·   One can only create sub-queries that return over one row with multiple value operators like IN and NOT IN operators.

· You cannot use a UNION in a sub-query. You are only allowed to use one SELECT statement.

· Your SELECT list should not include a reference to values testing to a BLOB, CLOB, ARRAY, or NCLOB.

· You cannot immediately enclose a sub-query within a set function.

· You cannot use the BETWEEN operator with a sub-query. However, you can use this operator within a sub-query.

Subqueries with SELECT Statement

In most cases, we use subqueries with the SQL's SELECT statement.

We do this using the syntax given below:

SELECT columnName [, columnName]

FROM   table_1 [, table_2]

WHERE columnName **OPERATOR**

   (**SELECT** columnName [,columnName]

   FROM table_1 [, table_2]

   [**WHERE**])

Consider the students table with the data given below:

Let us now create a query with a sub-query as shown below:

SELECT *

  FROM students

  WHERE regno **IN** (**SELECT** regno

    FROM students

    WHERE age >= 19);

The command should return the result given below:

We have used the following subquery:

SELECT regno

  FROM students

  WHERE age >= 19;

In the main query, we are using the results of the above subquery to return our final results. This means that the main query will only return the records of students whose age is 19 and above. That is what the above output shows.

Subqueries with INSERT Statement

We can also use Sub-queries with the INSERT statement. What happens, in this case, is that the insert statement will use the data that has been returned by the query to insert it into another table.

It is possible for us to change the data that the sub-query returns using date, character or number functions.

The following syntax shows how we can add a sub-query to the INSERT statement:

INSERT INTO tableName [(column_1 [, column_2])]

   SELECT [*|column_1 [, column_2]

   FROM table_1 [, table_2]

   [**WHERE** A **VALUE OPERATOR**]

Consider a situation in which we have the table students2 which is an exact copy of the **students'** table. First, let us create this table:

CREATE TABLE students2 **LIKE** students**;**

The table doesn't have even a single record. We need to populate it with data from the students' table. We then run the following query to perform this task:

INSERT INTO students2

   SELECT * **FROM** students

   WHERE regno **IN** (**SELECT** regno

   FROM students);

The code should run successfully as shown below:

We have used the regno column of the table named **students** to select all the records in that table and populate them into the table named **students2**. Let us query the table to see its contents:

It is clear that the table was populated successfully.

 Subqueries with UPDATE Statement

We can combine the update statement with a subquery. With this, we can update either single or multiple columns in a table.

We can do this using the following syntax:

UPDATE table

SET columnName = newValue

[**WHERE OPERATOR** [**VALUE**]

  (**SELECT** COLUMNNAME

  FROM TABLENAME)

  [**WHERE**)]

We need to show using the students' table. The table has the data given below:

> The table students2 is a copy of the students' table. We need to increase the ages of the students by 1. This means we run the following command:

UPDATE students

 SET age= age + 1

 WHERE regno **IN** (**SELECT** regno **FROM** students2);

The command should run successfully as shown below:

```
mysql> UPDATE students
    ->     SET age= age + 1
    ->     WHERE regno IN (SELECT regno FROM students2 );
Query OK, 5 rows affected (0.08 sec)
Rows matched: 5  Changed: 5  Warnings: 0

mysql>
```

Since the two tables have exactly the same data, all the records in the students' table were matched to the sub-query. This means that all the records were updated. To confirm this, we run a select statement against the students' table:

> The above figure shows that the values of age were increased by 1.

Subqueries with DELETE Statement

We can use sub-queries with the DELETE statement just like the other SQL statements. The following syntax shows how we can do this:

DELETE FROM TABLENAME

[**WHERE OPERATOR** [**VALUE**]

(**SELECT** COLUMNNAME

FROM TABLENAME)

[**WHERE**)]

Suppose we need to make a deletion on the students table. The students table has the following data:

The **students2** table is an exact copy of the above table as shown below:

We need to perform a deletion on the students table by running the following command:

DELETE FROM students

   WHERE AGE **IN** (**SELECT** age **FROM** students2

     WHERE AGE < 20);

The command should run successfully as shown below:

The record in which the value of age is below 20 will be deleted. This is because this is what the subqueries return. We can confirm this by running a select statement on the students' table as shown below:

The above output shows that the record was deleted successfully.

Chapter 8 Database Components

Now that you know more about a database's use in the real world and why you may want to learn SQL, we will dive into the components of the database.

These components or items within a database are typically referred to as "objects". These objects can range from tables, to columns, to indexes and even triggers. Essentially, these are all of the pieces of the data puzzle that make up the database itself.

The examples and screenshots used in the following sections are from the AdventureWorks2012 database, which you will be working with later on in this book.

Database Tables

Within the database are tables, which hold the data itself. A table consists of columns that are the headers of the table, like First_Name and Last_Name, for example. There are also rows, which are considered an entry within the table. The point to where the column and row intersect is called a cell.

The cell is where the data is shown, like someone's actual first name and last name. Some cells may not always have data, which is considered NULL in the database. This just means that no data exists in that cell.

In Microsoft's SQL Server, a table can have up to 1,024 columns, but can have any number of rows.

Schemas

A schema is considered a logical container for the tables. It's essentially, a way to group tables together based on the type of data that they hold. It won't affect an end user who interacts with the database, like someone who runs reports. But one who works directly with the database, like a database administrator or a developer, will see the available schemas.

Consider a realistic example of several tables containing data for Sales records. There may be several tables named Sales_Order, Sales_History or Sales_Customer. You can put all of these Sales tables into a "Sales" schema to better identify them when you work directly with the database.

Columns

Remember that you can only have up to 1,024 columns in a given table in SQL Server!

Rows and NULL values

A row is considered an entry in a table. The row will be one line across, and typically have data within each column. Though, in some cases, there may be a NULL value in one or many cells.

Back to our example of names, most people have first and last names, but not everyone has a middle name. In that case, a row would have values in the first and last name columns, but not the middle name column, like shown below.

Primary Keys

A primary key is a constraint on a column that forces every value in that column to be unique. By forcing uniqueness on values in that column, it helps maintain the integrity of the data and helps prevent any future data issues.

A realistic example of a primary key would be an employee ID or a sales record ID. You wouldn't want to have two of the same employee ID's for two different people, nor would you want to have two or more of the same sales record ID's for different sales transactions. That would be a nightmare when trying to store and retrieve data!

You can see in the below example that each value for BusinessEntityID is unique for every person.

Foreign Keys

Another key similar to the primary key is a foreign key. These differ from primary keys by not always being unique and act as a link between two or more tables.

Below is an example of a foreign key that exists in the AdventureWorks2012 database. The foreign key is ProductID in this table (Sales.SalesOrderDetail):

The ProductID in the above table is linking to the ProductID (primary key) in the Production.Product table:

Essentially, foreign keys will check its link to the other table to see if that value exists. If not, then you will end up receiving an error when trying to insert data into the table where the foreign key is.

Constraints

Primary keys and foreign keys are known as constraints in the database. Constraints are "rules" that are set in place as far as the types of data that can be entered. There are several others that are used aside from primary keys and foreign keys that help maintain the integrity of the data.

UNIQUE – enforces all values in that column to be different. An example of this could be applied to the Production.Product table. Each product should be different, since you wouldn't want to store the same product name multiple times.

NOT NULL – ensures that no value in that column is NULL. This could also be applied to the same table as above. In this case, the ProductNumber cannot have a NULL value, as each Product should have its own corresponding ProductNumber.

DEFAULT – sets a default value in a column when a value is not provided. A great example of this would be the ListPrice column. When a value isn't specified when being added to this table, the value will default to 0.00. If this value were to be calculated in another table and be a NULL value (like a sales table where sales from the company are made), then it would be impossible to calculate based on a NULL value since it's not a number. Using a default value of 0.00 is a better approach.

INDEXES – Indexes are constraints that are created on a column that speeds up the retrieval of data. An index will essentially compile all of the values in a column and treat them as unique values, even if they're not. By treating them as unique values, it allows the database engine to improve its search based on that column.

Indexes are best used on columns that:

- Do not have a unique constraint
- Are not a primary key
- Or are not a foreign key

The reason for not applying an index to a column that satisfies any of the above three conditions, is that these are naturally faster for retrieving data since they are constraints.

As an example, an index would be best used on something like a date column in a sales table. You may be filtering certain transaction dates from

January through March as part of your quarterly reports, yet see many purchases on the same day between those months. By treating it as a unique column, even the same or similar values can still be found much quicker by the database engine.

Views

A view is a virtual table that's comprised of one or more columns from one or more tables. It is created using a SQL query and the original code used to create the view is recompiled when a user queries that table.

In addition, any updates to data made in the originating tables (i.e. the tables and columns that make up the view) will be pulled into the view to show current data. This is another reason that views are great for reporting purposes, as you can pull real-time data without touching the origin tables.

For best practices, DO NOT update any data in a view. If you need to update the data for any reason, perform that in the originating table(s).

To expand a little bit on why a view would be used is the following:

1. To hide the raw elements of the database from the end-user so that they only see what they need to. You can also make it more cryptic for the end-user.

2. An alternative to queries that are frequently run in the database, like reporting purposes as an example.

These are only a few reasons as to why you would use a view. However, depending on your situation, there could be other reasons why you would use a view instead of writing a query to directly obtain data from one or more tables.

To better illustrate the concept of a view, the below example has two tables: 'People' and 'Locations'. These two tables are combined into a view that is called 'People and Locations' just for simplicity. These are also joined on a common field, i.e. the LocationID.

Stored Procedures

Stored procedures are pre-compiled SQL syntax that can be used over and over again by executing its name in SQL Server. If there's a certain query that you're running frequently and writing it from scratch or saving the file somewhere and then opening it to be able to run it, then it may be time to consider creating a stored procedure out of that query.

Just like with SQL syntax that you'd write from scratch and passing in a value for your WHERE clause, you can do the same with a stored procedure. You have the ability to pass in certain values to achieve the end result that you're looking for. Though, you don't always have to pass a parameter into a stored procedure.

As an example, let's say that as part of the HR department, you must run a query once a month to verify which employees are salary and non-salary, in compliance with labor laws and company policy.

Instead of opening a file frequently or writing the code from scratch, you can simply call the stored procedure that you saved in the database, to retrieve the information for you. You would just specify the proper value (where 1 is TRUE and 0 is FALSE in this case).

EXEC   **HumanResources.SalariedEmployees @SalariedFlag = 1**

In the result set below, you can see some of the employees who work in a salary type position:

Triggers

A trigger in the database is a stored procedure (pre-compiled code) that will execute when a certain event happens to a table. Generally, these triggers will fire off when data is added, updated or deleted from a table.

Below is an example of a trigger that prints a message when a new department is created in the HumanResources.Department table.

--Creates a notification stating that a new department has been created

--when an INSERT statement is executed against the Department table

> **CREATE TRIGGER** NewDepartment
> **ON** HumanResources.Department
> **AFTER INSERT**
>> **AS RAISERROR** ('A new department has been created.', *10, 9*)

To expand on this a little more, you specify the name of your trigger after CREATE TRIGGER. After ON, you'll specify the table name that this is associated with.

Next, you can specify which type of action will fire this trigger (you may also use UPDATE and/or DELETE), which is known as a DML trigger in this case.

Last, I'm printing a message that a new department has been created and using some number codes in SQL Server for configuration.

To see this trigger in the works, here's the INSERT statement I'm using to create a new department. There are four columns in this table, DepartmentID, Name, GroupName and ModifiedDate. I'm skipping the DepartmentID column in the INSERT statement because a new ID is automatically generated by the database engine.

<u>--Adding a new department to the Department's table</u>

INSERT INTO
HumanResources.Department
(**Name**, GroupName, ModifiedDate)

VALUES

('Business Analysis', 'Research and Development', GETDATE()) --GETDATE() gets the current date and time, depending on the data type being used in the table

The trigger will prompt a message after the new record has been successfully inserted.

A new department has been created.

(1 row(s) affected)

If I were to run a query against this table, I can see that my department was successfully added as well.

Deadlocks in SQL

In most of the cases, multiple users access database applications simultaneously, which means that multiple transactions are being executed on database in parallel. By default when a transaction performs an operation on a database resource such as a table, it locks the resource. During that period, no other transaction can access the locked resource. Deadlocks occur when two or more than two processes try to access resources that are locked by the other processes participating in the deadlock.

Deadlocks are best explained with the help of an example. Consider a scenario where some transactionA has performed an operation on tableA and has acquired lock on the table. Similarly, there is another transaction named transactionB that is executing in parallel and performs some operation on tableB. Now, transactionA wants to perform some operation on tableBwhich is already locked by transactionB. Similarly, transactionB wants to perform an operation on tableA, but it is already locked by transactionA. This results in a deadlock since transactionA is waiting on a resource locked by transactionB, which is waiting on a resource locked by transactionA. In this chapter we shall see a practical example of deadlocks. Then we will see how we can analyze and resolve deadlocks.

Dummy Data Creation

For the sake of this chapter, we will create a dummy database. This database will be used in the deadlock example that we shall in next section. Execute the following script

CREATE DATABASE dldb;

GO

```
USE dldb;

CREATE TABLE tableA
(
id INT IDENTITY PRIMARY KEY,
patient_name NVARCHAR(50)
)
INSERT INTO tableA VALUES ('Thomas')
CREATE TABLE tableB
(
id INT IDENTITY PRIMARY KEY,
patient_name NVARCHAR(50)
)
INSERT INTO table2 VALUES ('Helene')
```

The above script creates database named "dldb". In the database we create two tables: tableA and tableB. We then insert one record each in the both tables.

Practical Example of Deadlock

Let's write a script that creates deadlock. Open two instances of SQL server management studio. To simulate simultaneous data access, we will run our queries in parallel in these two instances.

Now, open the first instances of SSMS, and write the following script. Do not execute this script at the moment.

Instance1 Script

USE dldb;

BEGIN TRANSACTION transactionA

-- First update statement

UPDATE tableA SET patient name = 'Thomas - TransactionA'

WHERE id = 1

-- Go to the second instance and execute

-- first update statement

UPDATE tableB SET patient name = 'Helene - TransactionA'

WHERE id = 1

-- Go to the second instance and execute

-- second update statement

COMMIT TRANSACTION

In the second instance, copy and paste the following script. Again, do not run the Script.

Instance 2 Script

USE dldb;

BEGIN TRANSACTION transactionB

-- First update statement

UPDATE tableB SET patient name = 'Helene - TransactionB'

WHERE id = 1

-- Go to the first instance and execute

-- second update statement

UPDATE tableA SET patient name = 'Thomas - TransactionB'

WHERE id = 1

  COMMIT TRANSACTION

Now we have our scripts ready in both the transaction.

Open both the instances of SSMS side by side as shown in the following figure:

To create a deadlock we have to follow step by step approach. Go to the first instance of SQL Server management studio(SSMS) and execute the following lines from the script:

USE dldb;

BEGIN TRANSACTION transactionA

-- First update statement

UPDATE tableA SET patient name = 'Thomas - TransactionA'

171

WHERE id = 1

In the above script, transactionA updates the tableAby setting the name of the patient with id one to *'Thomas −TransactionA'*. At this point of time, transactionA acquires lock on tableA.

Now, execute the following script from the second instance of SSMS.

USE dldb;

BEGIN TRANSACTION transactionB

-- First update statement

UPDATE tableB SET patient name = 'Helene - TransactionB'

WHERE id = 1

The above script executes transactionB which updates tableB by setting the name of patient with id one to *'Helene − TransactionB'*, acquiring lock on tableB.

Now come back again to first instance of SSMS. Execute the following piece of script:

UPDATE tableB SET patient name = 'Helene - TransactionA'

WHERE id = 1

Here transactionA tries to update tableB which is locked by transactionB. Hence transactionA goes to waiting state.

Go to the second instance of SSMS again and execute the following piece of script.

UPDATE tableA SET patient name = 'Thomas - TransactionB'

WHERE id = 1

In the above script, transactionB tries to update tableA which is locked by transactionA. Hence transactionA also goes to waiting state.

At this point of time, transactionA is waiting for a resource locked by transactionB. Similarly, transactionB is waiting for the resource locked by TransactionA. Hence deadlock occurs here.

By default, SSMS selects one of the transactions involved in the deadlock as deadlock victim. The transaction selected as deadlock victim is rolled back, allowing the other transaction to complete its execution. You will see that after few second, the transaction in one of the instances will complete its execution while an error will appear in other instance.

In the example that we just saw, transactionA was allowed to complete its execution while transactionB was selected as deadlock victim. Your result can be different. This is shown in the following figure:

You can see the message "1 row affected" in the instance on the left that is running transactionA. On the other hand in the left instance an error is displayed that reads:

> Msg 1205, Level 13, State 51, Line 12
> Transaction (Process ID 54) was deadlocked on lock
> resources with another process and has been chosen

as the deadlock victim. Rerun the transaction.

The error says that the Transaction with process ID 54 was involved in a deadlock and hence chosen as victim of the deadlock.

Deadlock Analysis and Prevention

In the previous section we generated deadlock ourselves, therefore we have information about the processes involved in the deadlock. In the real world scenarios, this is not the case. Multiple users access the database simultaneously, which often results in deadlocks. However, in such cases we cannot tell which transactions and resources are involved in the deadlock. We need a mechanism that allows us to analyze deadlocks in detail so that we can see what transactions and resources are involved and decide how to resolve the deadlocks. One such ways is via SQL Server error logs.

Reading Deadlock info via SQL Server Error Log

The SQL Server provides only little info about the deadlock. You can get detailed information about the deadlock via SQL error log. However to log deadlock information to error log, first you have to use a trace flag 1222. You can turn trace flag 1222 on global as well as session level. To turn on trace flag 1222 on, execute the following script:

DBCC Traceon(1222, -1)

The above script turns trace flag on global level. If you do not pass the second argument, the trace flag is turned on session level. To see if trace flag is actually turned on, execute the following query:

DBCC TraceStatus(1222)

The above statement results in the following output:

TraceFlag	Status	Global	Session
1222	1	1	0

Here status value 1 shows that trace flag 1222 is on. The 1 for Global column implies that trace flag has been turned on globally.

Now, try to generate a deadlock by following the steps that we performed in the last section. The detailed deadlock information will be logged in the error log. To view sql server error log, you need to execute the following stored procedure.

executesp_readerrorlog

The above stored procedure will retrieve detailed error log a snippet of which is shown below:

Your error log might be different depending upon the databases in your database. The information about all the deadlocks in your database starts with log text "deadlock-list". You may need to scroll down a bit to find this row.

Let's now analyze the log information that is retrieved by the deadlock that we just created. Note that your values will be different for each column, but the information remains same.

ProcessInfo	Text
spid13s	deadlock-list
spid13s	deadlock victim=process1fcf9514ca8
spid13s	process-list
spid13s	process id=process1fcf9514ca8t

	askpriority=0 logused=308 waitresource=KEY: 8:72057594043105280 (8194443284a0) waittime=921 ownerId=388813 transactionname=trans actionBlasttranstarted= 2017-11- 01T15:51:46.547 XDES=0x1fcf8454490 lockMode=X schedulerid=3 kpid=1968 status=suspended spid=57 sbid=0 ecid=0 priority=0 trancount=2 lastbatchstarted=2017- 11-01T15:51:54.380 lastbatchcompleted=20 17-11- 01T15:51:54.377 lastattention=1900-01- 01T00:00:00.377 clientapp=Microsoft SQL Server Management Studio - Query hostname=DESKTOP-

	GLQ5VRA hostpid=968 loginname=DESKTOP-GLQ5VRA\Mani isolationlevel=read committed (2) xactid=388813 currentdb=8 lockTimeout=42949672 95 clientoption1=6710907 84 clientoption2=390200
spid13s	executionStack
spid13s	frame procname=adhoc line=2 stmtstart=58 stmtend=164 sqlhandle=0x02000000 14b61731ad79b1eec67 40c98aab3ab91bd31af4 d000000000000000000 0000000000000000000 000
spid13s	unknown
spid13s	frame procname=adhoc line=2 stmtstart=4 stmtend=142

	sqlhandle=0x02000000 80129b021f70641be5a 5e43a1ca1ef67e9721c9 7000000000000000000 0000000000000000000 000
spid13s	unknown
spid13s	inputbuf
spid13s	UPDATE tableA SET patient_name = 'Thomas - TransactionB'
spid13s	WHERE id = 1
spid13s	process id=process1fcf9515468 taskpriority=0 logused=308 waitresource=KEY: 8:72057594043170816 (8194443284a0) waittime=4588 ownerId=388767 transactionname=trans actionAlasttranstarted= 2017-11- 01T15:51:44.383 XDES=0x1fcf8428490 lockMode=X

	schedulerid=3
	kpid=11000
	status=suspended
	spid=54 sbid=0 ecid=0
	priority=0 trancount=2
	lastbatchstarted=2017-11-01T15:51:50.710
	lastbatchcompleted=2017-11-01T15:51:50.710
	lastattention=1900-01-01T00:00:00.710
	clientapp=Microsoft SQL Server Management Studio - Query
	hostname=DESKTOP-GLQ5VRA hostpid=1140
	loginname=DESKTOP-GLQ5VRA\Mani
	isolationlevel=read committed (2)
	xactid=388767
	currentdb=8
	lockTimeout=4294967295
	clientoption1=671090784
	clientoption2=390200

spid13s	executionStack
spid13s	frame procname=adhoc line=1 stmtstart=58 stmtend=164 sqlhandle=0x02000000 ec86cd1dbe1cd7fc9723 7a12abb461f1fc27e278 0000000000000000000 0000000000000000000 00
spid13s	unknown
spid13s	frame procname=adhoc line=1 stmtend=138 sqlhandle=0x02000000 3a45a10eb863d6370a5 f99368760983cacbf489 5000000000000000000 0000000000000000000 000
spid13s	unknown
spid13s	inputbuf
spid13s	UPDATE tableB SET patient_name = 'Helene - TransactionA'

spid13s	WHERE id = 1
spid13s	resource-list
spid13s	keylockhobtid=720575 94043105280　dbid=8 objectname=dldb.dbo.t ableAindexname=PK__t ableA__3213E83F1C2C 4D64 id=lock1fd004bd600 mode=X associatedObjectId=72 057594043105280
spid13s	owner-list
spid13s	owner id=process1fcf9515468 mode=X
spid13s	waiter-list
spid13s	waiter id=process1fcf9514ca8 mode=X requestType=wait
spid13s	keylockhobtid=720575 94043170816　dbid=8 objectname=dldb.dbo.t ableBindexname=PK__t ableB__3213E83FFE08

	D6AB id=lock1fd004c2200 mode=X associatedObjectId=72 057594043170816
spid13s	owner-list
spid13s	owner id=process1fcf9514ca8 mode=X
spid13s	waiter-list
spid13s	waiter id=process1fcf9515468 mode=X requestType=wait

The deadlock information logged by the SQL server error log has three main parts.

1-___The deadlock Victim

2-___Process List

The process list is the list of all the processes involved in a deadlock. In the deadlock that we generated, two processes were involved. In the processes list you can see details of both of these processes. The id of the first process is highlighted in red whereas the id of the second process is highlighted in green. Notice that in the process list, the first process is the process that has been selected as deadlock victim too.

Apart from process id, there you can also see other information about the processes. For instance, you can find login information of the process, the isolation level of the process etc. You can see the script that the process was trying to run. For instance if you look at the first process in the process list, you can find that it was trying to update the patient_name column of the table tableA, when the deadlock occurred.

3-___Resource List

The resource list contains information about the resources that were involved in the deadlock. In our example, tableA and tableB were the only two resources involved in the deadlock. You can both of these tables highlighted in blue in the resource list of the log in the table above.

Some tips for Deadlock Avoidance

From the error log we can get detailed information about the deadlock. However we can minimize the chance of deadlock occurrence if we follow these tips:

- *Execute transactions in a single batch and keep them short*

- *Release resources automatically after a certain time period*
- *Sequential resource sharing*
- Not allowing user to interact with the application when transactions are being executed.

This chapter presented a brief overview to deadlocks. In the next chapter, we shall see another extremely useful concept, i.e. Cursors.

Chapter 9 How to Manage Database Objects

This chapter will discuss database objects: their nature, behaviors, storage requirements, and interrelatedness. Basically, databases objects are the backbone of relational databases. You use these objects to store data (i.e. they are logical units found inside a database). For this reason, these objects are also called back-end databases.

What is a Database Object?

Database objects are the defined objects within a database utilized to save or retrieve information. Here are several examples of database objects: views, clusters, tables, indexes, synonyms, and sequences.

The Schema

A schema is a set of database objects linked to a certain database user. This user, known as the "schema owner," owns the set of objects linked to his/her username. Simply put, any person who generates an object has just generated his/her own schema. That means users have control over database objects that are generated, deleted, and manipulated.

Let's assume that you received login credentials (i.e. username and password) from a database administrator. The username is PERSON1. Let's say you accessed the database and created a table named EMPLOYEES_TBL. In the database's records, the file's actual name is PERSON1.EMPLOYEES_TBL. The table's "schema name" is PERSON1, which is also the creator/owner of that table.

When accessing a schema that you own, you are not required to use the schema name. That means you have two ways of accessing the imaginary file given above. These are:

- PERSON1.EMPLOYEES_TBL
- EMPLOYEES_TBL

As you can see, the second option involves fewer characters. This is the reason why schema owners prefer this method of accessing their files. If other users want to view the file, however, they must include the schema in their database query.

The screenshot below shows two schemas within a database.

Tables – The Main Tool for Storing Data

Modern database users consider tables as the main storage tool. In general, a table is formed by row/s and column/s. Tables take up space within a database and may be temporary or permanent.

Fields/Columns

Fields, referred to as columns when working with a relational database, are parts of a table where a particular data type is assigned to. You should name a field so that it matches the data type it will be used with. You may specify fields as NULL (i.e. nothing should be entered) or NOT NULL (i.e. something needs to be entered).

Each table should have at least one field. Fields are the elements inside a table that store certain kinds of data (e.g. names, addresses, phone numbers, etc.). For instance, you'll find a "customer name" column when checking a database table for customer information.

Rows

Rows are records of data within a table. For instance, a row in a customer database table might hold the name, fax number, and identification number of a certain customer. Rows are composed of fields that hold information from a single record in the table.

SQL Statement – CREATE TABLE

"CREATE TABLE" is an SQL statement used to generate a table. Even though you can create tables quickly and easily, you should spend time and effort in planning the structures of your new table. That means you have to do some research and planning before issuing this SQL statement.

Here are some of the questions you should answer when creating tables:

- What kind of data am I working on?
- What name should I choose for this table?
- What column will form the main key?
- What names should be assigned to the fields/columns?
- What type of data can be assigned to those columns?
- Which columns can be empty?
- What is the maximum length for every column?

Once you have answered these questions, using the CREATE TABLE command becomes simple.

Here's the syntax to generate a new table:

The final character of that statement is a semicolon. Almost all SQL implementations use certain characters to terminate statements or submit statements to the server. MySQL and Oracle use semicolons to perform these functions. Transact-SQL, on the other hand, utilizes the "GO" command. To make this book consistent, statements will be terminated or submitted using a semicolon.

The STORAGE Clause

Some SQL implementations offer STORAGE clauses. These clauses help you in assigning the table sizes. That means you can use them while creating tables. MySQL uses the following syntax for its STORAGE clause:

The Naming Conventions

When naming database objects, particularly columns and tables, you should choose names that reflect the data they will be used for. For instance, you may use the name EMPLOYEES_TBL for a table used to hold employee information. You need to name columns using the same principle. A column used to store the phone number of employees may be named PHONE_NUMBER.

SQL Command - ALTER TABLE

You can use ALTER TABLE, a powerful SQL command, to modify existing database tables. You may add fields, remove columns, change field definitions, include or exclude constraints, and, in certain SQL implementations, change the table's STORAGE values. Here's the syntax for this command:

Altering the Elements of a Database Table

A column's "attributes" refer to the laws and behaviors of data inside that column. You may change a column's attributes using ALTER TABLE. Here, the term "attributes" refers to:

- The type of data assigned to a column.
- The scale, length, or precision of a column.
- Whether you can enter NULL values into a column.

In the screenshot below, ALTER TABLE is used on the EMPLOYEE_TBL to change the attributes of a column named EMP_ID:

If you are using MySQL, you'll get the following statement:

Adding Columns to a Database Table

You must remember certain rules when adding columns to existing database tables. One of the rules is this: You can't add a NOT NULL column if the table has data in it. Basically, you should use NOT NULL to indicate that the column should hold some value for each data row within the table. If you'll add a NOT NULL column, you will go against this new constraint if the current data rows don't have specific values for the added column.

Modifying Fields/Columns

Here are the rules you should follow when altering existing columns:

- You can always increase a column's length.

- You can decrease a column's length only if the highest value for the column is lower than or equal to the desired length.
- You can always increase the quantity of digits for numeric data types.
- You can only decrease the quantity of digits for numeric data types if the value of the largest quantity of digits in the column is lower than or equal to the desired quantity of digits.
- You can increase or decrease the quantity of decimal places for numeric data types.
- You can easily change the data type of any column.

Important Note: Be extremely careful when changing or dropping tables. You might lose valuable information if you will commit typing or logical mistakes while executing these SQL statements.

How to Create New Tables from Existing Ones

You may duplicate an existing table using these SQL statements: (1) CREATE TABLE and (2) SELECT. After executing these statements, you'll get a new table whose column definitions are identical to that of the old one. This feature is customizable: you may copy all of the columns or just the ones you need. The columns generated using this pair of statements will assume the size needed to store the information. Here's the main syntax for generating a table from an existing one:

This syntax involves a new keyword (i.e. SELECT). This keyword can help you perform database queries. In modern database systems, SELECT can help you generate tables using search results.

How to Drop Tables

You can drop tables easily. If you used the RESTRICT statement and referenced the table using a view/constraint, the DROP command will give you an error message. If you used CASCASE, however, DROP will succeed and all constraints and/or views will be dropped. The syntax for dropping a table is:

Important Note: When dropping a database table, specify the owner or schema name of the table you are working on. This is important since dropping the wrong table can result to loss of data. If you can access multiple database accounts, make sure that you are logged in to the right account prior to dropping any table.

The Integrity Constraints

You can use integrity constraints to ensure the consistency and accuracy of data within a database. In general, database users handle integrity concerns through a concept called "Referential Integrity." In this section, you'll learn about the integrity constraints that you can use in SQL.

Primary Key

A primary key is used to determine columns that make data rows unique. You can form primary keys using one or more columns. For instance, either the product's name or an assigned reference number can serve as a primary key for a product table. The goal is to provide each record with a unique detail or primary key. In general, you can assign a primary key during table creation.

In the example below, the table's primary key is the column named EMP_ID.

You can assign primary keys this way while creating a new table. In this example, the table's primary key is an implicit condition. As an alternative, you may specify primary keys as explicit conditions while creating a table. Here's an example:

In the example given above, the primary key is given after the comma list.

If you need to form a primary key using multiple columns, you use this method:

Unique Column Constraint

Unique column constraints are similar to primary keys: the column should have a unique value for each row. While you need to place a primary key in a single column, you may place unique constraints on different columns. Here's an example:

In the example above, EMP_ID serves as the primary key. That means the column for employee identification numbers is being used to guarantee the uniqueness of each record. Users often reference primary key columns for database queries, especially when merging tables. The EMP_PHONE column has a unique value, which means each employee has a unique phone number.

Foreign Key

You can use this key while working on parent and child tables. Foreign keys are columns in a child table that points to a primary key inside the parent table. This type of key serves as the primary tool in enforcing referential integrity within a database. You may use a foreign key column to reference a primary key from a different table.

In the example below, you'll learn how to create a foreign key:

Here, EMP_ID serves as a foreign key for a table named EMPLOYEE_PAY_TBL. This key points to the EMP_ID section of another table (i.e. the EMPLOYEE_TBL table). With this key, the database administrator can make sure that each EMP_ID inside the EMPLOYEE_PAY_TBL has a corresponding entry in EMPLOYEE_TBL. SQL practitioners call this the "parent/child relationship."

Study the following figure. This will help you to understand the relationship between child tables and parent tables.

How to Drop Constraints

You can use the option "DROP CONSTAINT" to drop the constraints (e.g. primary key, foreign key, unique column, etc.) you applied for your tables. For instance, if you want to remove the primary key in a table named "EMPLOYEES", you may use this command:

Some SQL implementations offer shortcuts for removing constraints. Oracle, for instance, uses this command to drop a primary key constraint:

On the other hand, certain SQL implementations allow users to deactivate constraints. Rather than dropping constraints permanently, you may disable them temporarily. This way, you can reactivate the constraints you will need in the future.

Chapter 10 Database Advance Topics

In this chapter you will be introduced to some advance topics in SQL that goes beyond basic database transactions. Even if this section only includes an overview of cursors, triggers and errors, such knowledge could possibly help you extend the features of your SQL implementations.

Cursors

Generally, SQL commands manipulate database objects using set-based operations. This means that transactions are performed on a group or block of data. A cursor, on the other hand, processes data from a table one row at a time. It is created using a compound a statement and destroyed upon exit. The standard syntax for declaring a cursor is (which may differ for every implementation):

DECLARE CURSOR CURSOR_NAME IS {SELECT_STATEMENT}

You can perform operations on a cursor only after it has been declared or defined.

- Open a Cursor

Once declared, you perform an OPEN operation to access the cursor and then execute the specified SELECT statement. The results of the SELECT query will be saved in a certain area in the memory. The standard syntax for opening a cursor is:

OPEN **CURSOR_NAME**;

- Fetch Data from a Cursor

The FETCH statement is performed if you want to retrieve the query results or the data from the cursor. The standard syntax for fetching data is:

FETCH NEXT FROM **CURSOR_NAME** [INTO **FETCH_LIST**]

In SQL programming, the optional statement inside the square brackets will let you assign the data retrieved into a certain variable.

- Close a Cursor

There is a corresponding CLOSE statement to be executed when you open a particular cursor. Once the cursor is closed, all the names and resources used will be deallocated. Thus, the cursor is no longer available for the program to use. The standard syntax for closing a cursor is:

CLOSE **CURSOR_NAME**

Triggers

There are instances when you want certain SQL operations or transactions to occur after performing some specific actions. This scenario describes an SQL statement that triggers another SQL statement to take place. Essentially, a trigger is an SQL procedure that is compiled in the database that execute certain transactions based on other transactions that have previously occurred. Such triggers can be performed before or after the execution of DML statements (INSERT, DELETE and UPDATE). In addition, triggers can validate data integrity, maintain data consistency, undo transactions, log operations, modify and read data values in different databases.

- Create a Trigger

The standard syntax for creating a trigger is:

CREATE TRIGGER **TRIGGER_NAME**
            TRIGGER_ACTION_TIMETRIGGE
   R_EVENT
 ON TABLE_NAME
 [REFERENCING
OLD_OR_NEW_VALUE_ALIAS_LIST**]**
TRIGGERED_ACTION

TRIGGER_NAME - the unique identifying name for this object

TRIGGER_ACTION_TIMETRIGGER_EVENT - the specified time that the set of triggered actions will occur (whether before or after the triggering event).

TABLE_NAME – the table for which the DML statements have been specified

TRIGGERED_ACTION – specifies the actions to be performed once an event is triggered

Once a trigger has been created, it cannot be altered anymore. You can just either re-create or replace it.

How a trigger works depends what conditions you specify – whether it will fire at once when a DML statement is performed or it will fire multiple times for every table row affected by the DML statement. You can also include a threshold value or a Boolean condition, that when such condition is met will trigger a course of action.

- Drop a Trigger

The basic syntax for dropping a trigger is the same as dropping a table or a view:

DROP TRIGGER TRIGGER_NAME;

Errors

An error-free design or implementation is one of the ultimate goals in any programming language. You can commit errors by simply not following naming conventions, improperly writing the programming codes (syntax or typo errors like a missing apostrophe or parenthesis) or even when the data entered does not match the data type defined.

To make things easier, SQL has devised a way to return error information so that programmers will be aware of what is going on and be able to undertake the appropriate actions to correct the situation. Some of these error-handling mechanisms are the status parameter SQLSTATE and the WHENEVER clause.

- SQLSTATE

The status parameter or host variable SQLSTATE is an error-handling tool that includes a wide selection of anomalous condition. It is a string that consists of five characters (uppercase letters from A to Z and numerals from 0 to 9), where the first two characters refer to the class code while the next three is the subclass code. The class code identifies the status after an SQL statement has been completed – whether it is successful or not (if not successful, then one of the major types of error conditions are returned). Supplementary information about the execution of the SQL statement is also indicated in the subclass code.

The SQLSTATE is updated after every operation. If the value is '00000' (five zeroes), it means that the execution was successful and you can proceed to the next operation. If it contains a five-character string other than '00000', then you have to check your programming lines to rectify the error committed. There are numerous ways on how to handle a certain SQL error, depending on the class code and subclass code specified in the SQLSTATE.

- WHENEVER Clause

The WHENEVER clause error-handling mechanism focuses on execution exceptions. With this, an error is acknowledged and gives the programmer the option to correct it. This is better than not being able to do something if an error occurs. If you cannot rectify or reverse the error that was committed, then you can just gracefully terminate the application program.

*WHENEVER **CONDITION ACTION**;*

> **CONDITION** – value can either be SQLERROR (returns TRUE if SQLSTATE class code is other than 00, 01 or 02) or NOT FOUND (returns TRUE if SQLSTATE is 02000)
>
> **ACTION** – value can either be CONTINUE (execution of the program is continued normally) or GOTO address (execution of a designated program address)

In this chapter you have learnt the primary role of cursors, how triggers work and the importance of handling errors in SQL programming. Learning these advance topics is one step closer in maximizing the potentials of your SQL implementations.

Chapter 11 Clauses and Queries

In this chapter we'll be dealing with clauses and queries. A query, is, simply put, a set of instructions you give in order to change a table within a database. The ones we will be looking at in this chapter are primarily the UPDATE and DELETE queries.

While you should have learned about other queries prior to reading this book, these two are the building blocks of any SQL developer worth their salt.

Both of these queries are very self-explanatory. The UPDATE query will take the information currently within a table, and change it to whatever you desire. The DELETE query is quite like an UPDATE query just with "null" instead of what you wanted to change it to. It will delete any entries that you wish.

It is important to note that while these queries are extremely important, they're also inefficient. You'll learn later on that there are much more efficient ways to do what these queries do, and at a much larger scale.

With that being said, they are still a must-learn for budding developers. They help you learn the fundamental blocks that advanced SQL is based on. After all, every business owner has heard horror stories of developers that only know higher-level material, and low-level techniques become their downfall.

These queries will primarily be useful in debugging and lower-level positions. Otherwise, they're only useful for manually editing smaller tables, at which point you might as well use Excel instead of SQL.

On the other side of the coin, we have the TOP query. The TOP query, rather than actually changing the information inside a table, shows you only specific entries from a table. To be precise, the TOP query will show you the topmost N or topmost N % of a given table.

This is especially useful if you're using SQL for maths or science, in which case it can make recurring certain functions very easy.

Besides that, this chapter will also cover the LIKE and ORDER BY clauses. The LIKE clause is meant to compare different objects/strings while the ORDER BY clause will sort a table in ascending or descending order, as you feel fit.

These are two extremely powerful tools that you'll use throughout your career as a SQL developer, so let's dive right in!

 UPDATE & DELETE Query

The UPDATE query in SQL is mainly intended to be used when modifying the records that are already in a table. What's worth noting here is that if you use the WHERE clause together with the UPDATE query, only the rows you selected with the WHERE clause will be updated. If you don't do this, then every row inside the table will be equally affected.

The Syntax for an UPDATE query within a WHERE clause is:

UPDATE name_of_table

SET column01 = value01, column02=value02…, columnN = valueN

WHERE[your_condition];

When using the UPDATE query, you'll be able to combine any N number of conditions by using the two operators you should be familiar with already: the AND and OR operators.

Take this for example:

In the following table, there are customer records listed, and you're trying to update the record.

You can combine N number of conditions using the AND or the OR operators.

```
+--+----------+-----+-----------+----------+
| ID | NAME     | AGE | ADDRESS   | SALARY   |
+--+----------+-----+-----------+----------+
|  1 | Ilija    |  19 | Uruguay   | 1500.00  |
|  2 | Frank    |  52 | France    |  200.00  |
```

```
| 3 | Jim       | 53 | Serbia    | 8040.00 |
| 4 | Martinia| 54 | Amsterdam| 9410.00 |
| 5 | Jaffar    | 66 | Podgorica | 55200.00 |
| 6 | Tim       | 33 | Prune     | 1200.00 |
| 7 | Kit       | 24 | England   | 700.00 |
+--+----------+-----+-----------+----------+
```

Let's say you want to update the address of the customer with the ID number 2, you would do it as such:

SQL> UPDATE CUSTOMER

SET ADDRESS = 'Tom_St'

WHERE ID = 2;

Now, the CUSTOMERS table would have the following records —

```
+--+----------+-----+-----------+----------+
| ID | NAME     | AGE | ADDRESS   | SALARY  |
+--+----------+-----+-----------+----------+
| 1 | Ilija     | 19 | Uruguay   | 1500.00 |
| 2 | Frank     | 52 | Tom_St    | 200.00 |
| 3 | Jim       | 53 | Serbia    | 8040.00 |
| 4 | Martinia| 54 | Amsterdam| 9410.00 |
| 5 | Jaffar    | 66 | Podgorica | 55200.00 |
```

```
| 6 | Tim      | 33 | Prune      | 1200.00 |
| 7 | Kit      | 24 | England    | 700.00 |
+--+----------+-----+-----------+----------+
```

Now, if instead, let's say you want to change the salaries and addresses of all your customers, then you won't need to use the WHERE clause. The UPDATE query will handle it all by itself. This can sometimes save quite a bit of time, let's look at the following example:

SQL> UPDATE CUSTOMER

SET ADDRESS = 'Tom_St', SALARY = 1000.00;

Now, CUSTOMERS table would have the following records −

```
+--+----------+-----+-----------+----------+
| ID | NAME    | AGE | ADDRESS   | SALARY  |
+--+----------+-----+-----------+----------+
| 1 | Ilija    | 19 | Tom_St    | 1000.00 |
| 2 | Frank    | 52 | Tom_St    | 1000.00 |
| 3 | Jim      | 53 | Tom_St    | 1000.00 |
| 4 | Martinia | 54 | Tom_St | 1000.00 |
| 5 | Jaffar   | 66 | Tom_St   | 1000.00 |
| 6 | Tim      | 33 | Tom_St    | 1000.00 |
| 7 | Kit      | 24 | Tom_st    | 1000.00 |
```

```
+--+----------+-----+----------+----------+
```

If you can't really tell where this would be useful, don't worry. There are countless examples from around the corporate world. This will let you replace any given thing in a matter of minutes. While it might not seem practical in a table with 7 people in it, imagine you're Microsoft and instead of 4 columns and 7 rows, you have 50 columns and 7000 rows, that isn't very practical to do by hand now is it?

Now let's take a look at the DELETE query. You can probably imagine what it does. It helps you delete certain records from a table. Now, obviously you don't want your whole table gone, so you should probably use the WHERE clause together with it, so you don't accidentally end up deleting, well, everything. When you use the WHERE clause with the DELETE query, only what you've selected will be deleted. Kind of like clicking on a file and pressing delete on your keyboard.

Let's turn our eyes to the syntax a bit, let's use the customers example again for it.

DELETE FROM name_of_table

WHERE [your_condition];

Similarly to the UPDATE query, you can use this in conjunction with the OR and AND operators to get more complex and precise results. Let's look at the past example we used:

```
+--+----------+-----+-----------+----------+
| ID | NAME | AGE | ADDRESS   | SALARY   |
+--+----------+-----+-----------+----------+
|  1 | Ilija     |  19 | Tom_St   |  1000.00 |
|  2 | Frank     |  52 | Tom_St   |  1000.00 |
|  3 | Jim       |  53 | Tom_St   |  1000.00 |
|  4 | Martinia  |  54 | Tom_St   |  1000.00 |
|  5 | Jaffar    |  66 | Tom_St   |  1000.00 |
|  6 | Tim       |  33 | Tom_St   |  1000.00 |
|  7 | Kit       |  24 | Tom_st   |  1000.00 |
+--+----------+-----+-----------+----------+
```

Let's say you want to erase a customer. Maybe they stopped shopping at your locale? Moved to a different state? Whatever reason it may be, this is how you could do it, let's say the customer's number is 7.

SQL> DELETE FROM CUSTOMER

WHERE ID = 7;

As you can see, this is quite similar to the UPDATE query, and they really are similar. If you need some help in thinking about the DELETE query, think about it as an UPDATE query that updates with empty spaces (this isn't entirely accurate, but it helps).

Now the customers table would look like this:

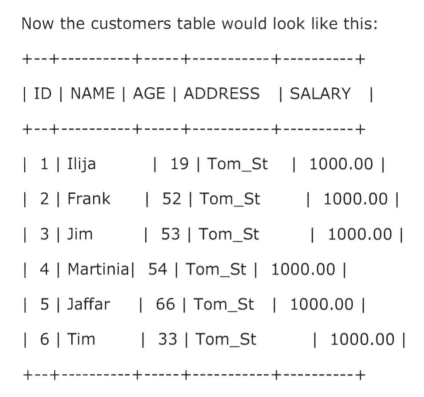

```
+--+----------+-----+-----------+----------+
| ID | NAME | AGE | ADDRESS   | SALARY  |
+--+----------+-----+-----------+----------+
| 1 | Ilija      | 19 | Tom_St  | 1000.00 |
| 2 | Frank    | 52 | Tom_St   | 1000.00 |
| 3 | Jim       | 53 | Tom_St    | 1000.00 |
| 4 | Martinia| 54 | Tom_St | 1000.00 |
| 5 | Jaffar    | 66 | Tom_St  | 1000.00 |
| 6 | Tim       | 33 | Tom_St     | 1000.00 |
+--+----------+-----+-----------+----------+
```

As you can see, all that changed is the 7th column is now empty. If you've been wondering how it would look if you hadn't used the WHERE operator, this is how:

```
+--+----------+-----+-----------+----------+
+--+----------+-----+-----------+----------+
```

That's right! Using the DELETE query without a WHERE operator results in an empty table.

Now, hopefully you won't be using the DELETE query too much wherever you end up working, but it can be useful for a variety of things. For example, when your company is moving servers, or simply purging outdated entries.

Like & Order by Clause

The LIKE clause is utilized when you want to compare two different values. This is done using wildcard operators such as the percent sign and the underscore. Now, while these are the only wildcard operators which are used with the LIKE clause, you'll encounter many more throughout this book.

First, the percentage symbol (%) serves to represent 0, 1 or N characters. Meanwhile the underscore (_) is used to represent only a single digit or symbol. You can also choose to combine these two when it suits you.

The syntax for using the percentage and underscore signs is:

1. - SELECT FROM name_of_table

    WHERE column LIKE '%NNNN%'

2. - SELECT FROM name_of_table

    WHERE column LIKE 'NNNN%'

3. - SELECT FROM name_of_table

    WHERE column LIKE 'NNNN_'

4. - SELECT FROM name_of_table

    WHERE column LIKE '_NNNN'

5. - SELECT FROM name_of_table

   WHERE column LIKE '_NNNN_'

So, to summarize, it doesn't matter whether you put the underscore or percentage symbol on one side of the "NNNN" or on both, as long as they're present.

NNNN here can be any string or numerical value, and you can combine any N conditions by utilizing the OR and AND operators.

When it comes to the ORDER BY clause, that is usually utilized when you need to sort the data ascendingly or descendingly. This will be done by basing it off of 1-N columns. Keep in mind though, that some databases have an ORDER BY clause set as ascending by default.

When it comes to the syntax for the ORDER BY clause, it's a bit more complex than those we've looked at so far, so make sure to pay good attention to it. The syntax is:

SELECT list-column

FROM name_of_table

[WHERE your condition]

[ORDER BY column01, column02, .. column0N] [ASC | DESC];

Keep in mind you can use more than a single column with the ORDER BY clause. It's possible to manipulate and access any N columns at the same time. It's important to ascertain that whichever column you're currently sorting is the column that should be in the list-column.

Let us consider the previous customer example once again:

```
+--+----------+-----+-----------+----------+
| ID | NAME | AGE | ADDRESS   | SALARY  |
+--+----------+-----+-----------+----------+
|  1 | Ilija      | 19 | Tom_St   | 1500.00 |
|  2 | Frank    | 52 | Tom_St   | 1300.00 |
|  3 | Jim       | 53 | Tom_St   | 1200.00 |
|  4 | Martinia| 54 | Tom_St | 1900.00 |
|  5 | Jaffar    | 66 | Tom_St   | 1000.00 |
|  6 | Tim       | 33 | Tom_St   | 1000.00 |
|  7 | Kit        | 24 | Tom_st   | 1000.00 |
+--+----------+-----+-----------+----------+
```

You might want to sort your customers in ascending order by their names and salary. You might want to do this so you can know which ones pay the most and which pay the least, so you can later make informed decisions about this, you would do it as follows:

SQL> SELECT * FROM CUSTOMER

ORDER BY NAME, SALARY;

If you did this, you would get a result where Jaffar is first, Jim 2nd and so on. Although it would also take salary into consideration, so the list may not be precisely as you would expect.

On the other hand, if you simply wanted to sort by name, that would look like:

SQL> SELECT * FROM CUSTOMER

ORDER BY NAME;

The ORDER BY clause is extremely important to remember, as sorting and order play a heavy hand in many programs.

TOP

The TOP clause in SQL does just what it says on the tin. It will output the top N or N percent of entries from a given table. This can make it useful when organizing data, as most of the time you won't need every single data point.

An important thing to notice here is that not all databases use the TOP clause. MySQL will use LIMIT in its place, doing functionally the same thing as a TOP clause does in regular SQL. Oracle also uses the ROWNUM command to do the exact same thing.

All in all, just remember to check which database you're using before using the TOP clause, as one of its relatives may be more appropriate.

The essential syntax for the TOP clause, with a necessary SELECT statement, is:

SELECT TOP number|percent name_of_column(s)

FROM name_of_table

WHERE [your_condition]

Returning back to the familiar customer example, here's how you would separate the top 3 from the following table:

```
+--+----------+-----+-----------+----------+
| ID | NAME     | AGE | ADDRESS   | SALARY   |
+--+----------+-----+-----------+----------+
|  1 | Ilija    |  19 | Uruguay   |  1500.00 |
|  2 | Frank    |  52 | France    |   200.00 |
|  3 | Jim      |  53 | Serbia    |  8040.00 |
|  4 | Martinia|  54 | Amsterdam|  9410.00 |
|  5 | Jaffar   |  66 | Podgorica | 55200.00 |
|  6 | Tim      |  33 | Prune     |  1200.00 |
|  7 | Kit      |  24 | England   |   700.00 |
+--+----------+-----+-----------+----------+
```

SQL> SELECT TOP 3 * FROM CUSTOMERS;

The output of this would be:

```
+--+----------+-----+-----------+----------+
```

```
| ID | NAME     | AGE | ADDRESS   | SALARY   |
+--+----------+-----+-----------+----------+
| 1 | Ilija    | 19 | Urugu     | 1500.00 |
| 2 | Frank    | 52 | France    | 200.00 |
| 3 | Jim      | 53 | Serbia    | 8040.00 |
+--+----------+-----+-----------+----------+
```

Now, the TOP clause isn't used very often in business. With that being said, it can sometimes be useful when it comes to mathematics and sciences. Many mathematical functions rely on finding the first X numbers of a sequence and doing something to them. You could separate these using a TOP clause with ease.

While it isn't the most useful clause, it is nonetheless necessary to learn in order to progress as an SQL developer.

Conclusion

With this, we have come to the end of this book. I thank you once again for choosing this book.

In today's world, there is a lot of data that is made available to you. If you own a business or want to start a business, you must know how to take care of the data you collect and use that information to improve the functioning of the business. You should also learn to store the information in one location, to ensure that you can access it whenever necessary. Whether you are trying to hold on to the personal information of your customers in one place or you are more interested in putting the sales information in an easy to look at way, you need to have a database that is easy to use.

In this guidebook, we are going to spend some time talking about SQL and how you can use it in a manner that will help you to deal with all your data management needs. SQL is a simple language that can help you analyze your data regardless of the type of business you run. We are going to cover some of the basic information you need to make this system work for you.

There is so much that you can learn about when it comes to SQL and using this system to make your business more successful. This guidebook is going to help you to get started so that you can organize and access your data any time you want to.

COMPUTER PROGRAMMING JAVASCRIPT:

Introduction

If there is anything, I want you to hold at the end of this programming guide for JavaScript is the fact that:

- JavaScript is the HTML and web language
- *It is easy to Learn*

If you can do that, then at the end, you will smile your way to programming for the web. However, your speed in learning JavaScript and other programming language is very dependent on you. If you find yourself struggling, don't feel demoralized rather take a break and reread the material after you have settled down. Remember, this chapter gives you the basics of JavaScript as a beginner to familiarize yourself with the language.

Variables in JavaScript

```
var exam = 50;

var test = 12;

var score = exam * test;
```

In the example above, exam, test, and score are variables given values with the value stored. We can perform various operations in JavaScript including multiplication, subtraction, addition, subtraction, and division. Variables and values can be declared as a number, string, or letter.

```
var name = "insert your name";

var number = '45';
```

From the example, you can enclose string with a single or double quote because they work exactly the same way.

JavaScript Identifiers

Every variable in JavaScript must have a unique name, which is used to identify it. These unique names are called identifiers. Identifiers have certain rules, which include:

- Every identifier must begin with a letter
- They can contain digits (0-9), letters (a-z), dollar signs ($), and underscores (_)
- Reserved words are not accepted
- Variable names are case sensitive
- *An identifier can begin with a dollar sign or underscore.*

Scope of JavaScript Variable

JavaScript allows two types of variable scope, which includes global and local variable scope. A variable is said to be global if it is declared outside the function body. With this, every statement has access to the variable within the same document. However, a local variable scope has its scope within the function. With this, the variable is only available to statements within the same function.

Basic JavaScript on the Browser side

When you hear about JavaScript on the browser side, it refers to the client-side, which means the code is run on the machine of the client – the browser. The browser-side components comprise of JavaScript, JavaScript libraries, CSS, images, HMTL, and whatever files downloaded to the browser.

Browser-Side JavaScript Features

JavaScript is important for the web as it is likely to use it to write programs that execute arbitrary computations. You have the opportunity of writing simple scripts such as the search for prime numbers or Fibonacci numbers. However, in the context of web browser and the Web, JavaScript enables programmers to program with the capability of computing sales tax, based on the information provided by the users through an HTML form.

The truth about JavaScript language is in the document-based objects and browser that the language is compatible with. This may sound complex, however, I will explain the significant capabilities of JavaScript on the browser side along with the objects it supports.

- *Controls the Browser* – There are various JavaScript objects that permit the control of the browser behavior. Furthermore, the Window object support means of popping up dialog boxes that display messages for the users. Additionally, users can also input messages. Besides this, JavaScript doesn't provide a method that gives users the opportunity to directly create and manipulate frames inside the browser window. Notwithstanding, you can take advantage of the ability to make HTML animatedly by creating the particular frame layout you want.
- *Interact with HTML Forms* – another significant part of the JavaScript on the browser side is its capability to work together with HTML forms. The ability comes because of the form element and its objects, which contains Text, submit, select, reset, radio, hidden, password, and text area objects. With these elements, you can write and read the values of the elements in the form.

- Interact with Users – *JavaScript has another feature, which is its ability to define event handlers. Most times, users initiate these events. For instance, when someone moves the mouse through a hyperlink, clicks the submit button, or enters a value. The capability to handle such events is important because programming with graphic interfaces requires an event-driven model.*

In addition to these aforementioned features, JavaScript on the browser side has other capabilities such as:

- Changing the displayed image by using the <img> tag to generate an animation effect and image rollover
- It has a window.setTimeout () method, which allows some block of random source code to be performed in the future within a split of a second
- It streamlines the procedure of working and computing with times and dates

JavaScript Framework

Take a moment and consider creating a web application and websites like constructing a house. In building a house, you can decide to create every material you need to start the house from scratch before building without any plans. This will be time-consuming and won't make much sense. One thing you may likely do is to buy pre-manufactured materials such as bricks, woods, countertops, etc. before assembling them based on the blueprint you have.

Coding is like taking it upon yourself to build a house. When you begin coding a website, you can code all areas of the site from scratch without. However, there are certain website features, which gives your website more sense by applying a template. Assuming you want to buy a wheel, it will make to look for one that you can reinvent. This is where JavaScript Frameworks come to the scene.

JavaScript Framework is a collection of JavaScript code libraries, which gives website developers pre-written JavaScript codes to use for their routine programming tasks and features.

You can also refer to it as an application framework, which is written in JavaScript where the developers can manipulate the functions of these codes and reuse them for their own convenience. They are more adaptable for website designing, which is why many developers use them in building websites.

Top JavaScript Framework

Vue.js

This is one of the JavaScript frameworks, which was created to make the user interface development more organized. Created by Evan You, it is the perfect JavaScript framework for beginners because it's quite easy to understand. Furthermore, it focuses on view layers. With Vue.js, you don't need Babel. A Babel is a transpiler with the responsibility of converting JavaScript codes to the old version of ES5 that can run in all browsers. All templates in the Vue.js framework are valid HTML, which makes their integration easier. If you want to develop lightweight apps as a beginner, it is best to start with Vue.js.

Next.js

Another important JavaScript Framework is the Next.js framework, which is an additional tool for server-side rendering. The framework allows developers to simplify the developing process similar to the Vue.js framework.

The features of this JavaScript Framework include page-based client-side routing and automatic splitting of codes. The framework also comes with a full CSS support, which makes styling of the user's interface easier for beginners and professionals.

Ember.js

This framework, which was created a few years ago, is among the most sought JavaScript framework in the web industry. Famous companies such as LinkedIn, Heroku, and Kickstarter use the Ember.js framework in the design of their websites. It also comes with regular updates and offers a complete feature for users. Unlike the Vue.js framework, it is effective for developers who want to develop complex web applications. The focus of this framework is on scalability, which allows developers to use it for both web and mobile projects.

Angular

Google released this JavaScript Framework in 2010 with regular updates and improvements taking place. It is one of the most sought after the framework for many developers because it simplifies the development of websites and apps. For other developers, it is because of its ability to create dynamic web apps.

Chapter 1. Use of a Global Variable as a Cache

In cases where a small app is to be created and in which one will incur an overhead when trying to integrate the app with a third-party mechanism, these can easily be handled inside the Node.js app, and this should be executed in the mode for a single thread.

In this mode, that is, the single threaded mode, a single application is executed at a time, and this is responsible for handling all of the requests sent to it. This is similar to what happens with desktop allocations. Other web apps developed by use of other programming languages for web development such as PHP, Ruby, and Python do not function in this manner. A global variable can be defined in this case, and this will become accessible to all of the requests that we make. This needs to be considered with a lot of concern.

For this mechanism to be achieved, one can create global variables of the necessary type and then a manipulation mechanism should be added inside this function. This will make it persist inside all of our requests.

Consider the code given below, which shows how this can be done effectively:

```
'use strict';

//this should be the cache for the js file

var  cache = {};

exports.someMethod = function(data){

/*The business logic should be added here*/

//setting the cache

cache[key] = val;

//retrieving the cache

cVal = cache[key];

//deleting the cache

delete cache[key];

/*The business logic should be added here*/
```

Logging without the use of a third-part Library

Whenever we want to print temporary information, we use the "*console.log*" so as to log in to the system. In the deployment stage, there are good libraries which can be used for this purpose. Some people hate the idea of using third-party libraries so as to log into their node.js app. However, this has been solved by the provision of an alternative. With the native support, one can be availed with a very decent mechanism for logging into their node.js app.

The Node.js's console object provides us with different levels of logging. These need to be used in the way they were designed to be used, otherwise, you will have trouble in using them. When you want to execute your node app, you should specify a logfile in which you will need to have everything written. This can be done as shown in the command given below:

$node app.js > mylogfile.log

After executing the above command, you will be set. The information about logging will be kept in the above file, and you will be in a position to view it later when you want to gain insight into some useful or critical information. It is also good for security purposes.

Whenever we want to print something on our console terminal, we should use the format given below:

console.log("The value of my variable should be:"+xyz);

This should only work for items which are single valued. If it was a json object, then we could have used *"console.log(xyz)."* This shows that the + operator does not work in this case.

About the use of "*"

It is recommended that this should not be used in a production dependency. Most people use it in their package.json file so as to specify the version or to use the "*" so that they can always have the latest package with them. One should have all of their packages updated to the latest version, since it might have some bug fixes, several improvements, and even new features added to it. However, this is only good for those whose product is in the development stage but has not reached the production stage.

In case of compatibility errors, fixing it will be easy. This is shown in the code given below:

//other of this:

"dependencies": {

"clustered-node": "*"

//use the following

"dependencies": {

"clustered-node": "~0.0.10"

For those who use such notations in a production environment, this is very risky. This is because one will not know when and which package might break and crash the application, which is possible. This is why it should only be used in the development phase, but once the product gets into the production environment, you should switch to dependencies which are based on a specific version. This should be done during the deployment phase of the product.

Asynchronous looping

Whenever we use the AsyncJS/underscoreJS in asynchronous flow looping/control, we get very useful and essential support. For those who know more about the callback concept, they can use it in a very native manner. If you are not interested in using this library in a simple task, then use the mechanism given in the code below. Here is the code:

```
var iterate = function(items, it){

console.log("Now handling: "+it);

//async methods

someAsyncMethod(parameterss,                function callback(){

if(items.length <= it)return;

return iterate(items, ++it);

})

};

var items = [5, 6, 7, 8];

iterate(items, 0);
```

Chapter 2. The Basics of JavaScript Function and Scope

Let's see now, normally when we are talking about a 'function' what's the first thing that comes to your mind? Obviously an activity right?

The functions in JavaScript also work in a similar manner. Functions are blocks of codes which are required to be executed over and over again by the program. A Function is used to perform a particular task. A Function can contain any number of arguments and statements; they can even have none. Depending on how the structure is coded, it may or may not return any value to the user.

A Function is declared in the following manner:

Function name(   ) { /*code blocks to be executed*/}

To start the Function, we start with the function keyword, and then we add the *name,* and parentheses. To finish the function, we place the code blocks to be executed in a curvy brackets.

You can also put the function in a named variable-

var jam = function() {/* code blocks to be executed*/}

Below are few examples of how you can execute a function-

i) **This is the example of the most basic function**

```
varsayHello = function(person, greeting) {

var text = greeting + ` , `+ person;

console.log(text);

};

Say Hello (` Jessica` , ` Hello`);
```

ii) **This is the example of a function that returns a value**

var greet = function (person, greeting)

{

 var writing = greeting + ` , ` + person ;

 return function () {console.log(text); };

}

console.log(greet(`Richard` ,` Hello"));

iii) **Sometimes, you might want to use a nested function. (Note: A nested function is a function within another function.)**

varsayHi = function(person, greeting) {

```
var text = greeting + ',' + person;

return function() {console.log (text);}

};

var greeting = greet( ' Richard' , 'Hello');
greeting();
```

Self-Executing Anonymous Function
Programmers have always been looking for the most advanced and clever methods available to improve their programming experience and ways to make it more accessible and easier for them. This resulted in the creation of the*Self-Executing Anonymous function*.

The core purpose of the self-executing anonymous function is to create a JavaScript function and then immediately execute it upon its conception.

This makes it much easier for a programmer who isworking on large scale programs. Likewise, it will help you to code without creating a messy global namespace.

A basic Self-Executing Anonymous Function Would be-

It is very important that you understand how to use this type of function if you plan on programming complex code in JavaScript. Using the Self-Executing Anonymous Function can produce some great code that is easy to use. As an example, the

JQuery library is designed to make using JavaScript on websites much easier. It does this by wrapping the entire library in one large self-executing function.

Typeof Operator

You might run into a situation where you need to determine the type of variable that you are working in JavaScript. You won't have call Sherlock Holmes to find that! Instead, you can simply use the 'typeof' operator to determine the type of any specific value. In other words, the typeof operator is used to evaluate the type of the operand.

EX-

Varmyvar=0

alert(typeofmyvar) *//alerts "number"*
Number isn't the only type of operand that can be detected. It can also be: string, Boolean, object, null, and not defined.

Scope

Scope is the accessibility of a variable.
A good understanding of Scope is necessary when it comes to debugging because it allow you to know what variable from which code block is causing the problem.

The simple rule here is that whenever you declare a variable inside a scope, it will only be recognized by the statements that are inside that scope; the statements that are outside the scope will not acknowledge its existence and so that variable will not work.

Another way to look at this is to imagine your entire code as a hotel with specific functions and sections of code as hotel rooms. The hotel rooms represent the private scopes of the code, while the common areas represent the global scope. A person in one hotel room cannot see or use what is in another hotel room. Staff who work in the hotel (and the global scope) also don't have access to private hotel rooms unless they have specific permission. Meanwhile, guests can go through the common areas and make use of any object there.

Thus, you can see how scope can affect how your code runs. If you need two different functions to access the same variable, you need to ensure that they both have access to it. One key way to ensure that the necessary variables have access to is to make your variables globally accessible.

There are two possible alternatives if you want your variables to become globally accessible.

The first thing you can do is to declare the variable outside the scope of your given piece of code, this will allow any functions in your program to be able to call it and recognize it.

The other thing you can do is to declare the variables inside your scope without using the word var. If the same variable was not defined at the beginning of the code outside the scope of the piece of code in question, then the variable will act similarly to a global one.

Ex-

```
var foo = 'hello';

var talkHello = function() {

console.log(foo);

};

talkHello(); // logs 'hello'

console.log(foo); // also logs 'hello'
```

As you can see, the variable foo is declared outside of the function talkHello. That means that foo is a global variable and any function will be able to access it, so when the function talkHello calls it, it is accessible.

The following example is contradictory to the first example. This shows that a code block that was written outside the scope is not being able to recognize the variable.

```
var talkHello = function() {

var doo = 'hello';

console.log(doo);

};
```

talkHello(); // logs 'hello'

console.log(doo); // gives an empty log.

In this example, the variable doo is called inside the function talkHello. This creates a private variable that is only accessible to the function, hence when the command console.log(doo) attempts to access it, it returns a null value.

Some Common Mistakes to Avoid

☐ Always remember that a variable is only accessible by the functions within a specific scope, outside of that scope the variable is invalid.

Practice

☐ Explain what a scope is and how the variables are affected by it.

☐ Write a simple program to illustrate the functionalities of a:-

a) Simple Function

b) A Function with returnable value

c) A function passed as a parameter (Argument)

☐ Explain the concept of a Self-Executing Anonymous Function and give an example.

Chapter 3. Loop Constructs

Looping is another fundamental programming construct that most programming languages support. Fundamentally, looping is used to execute the same set of statements iteratively until a condition remains true. JavaScript supports four types of looping constructs.

While Loop

The most basic loop construct is the while loop. This type of a loop executes the set of statements inside the while loop until the expression for the while is true. As soon as the expression becomes false, the while loop execution terminates. The syntax for implementation of while is given below –

while (expression){

//Statements of the while block

}

Sample implementation of the while loop is given below –

<html>

<body>

<script type="text/javascript">

```
<!--
var c = 0;
document.write("Loop begins...");
while (c < 5){
document.write("Value  of  c:  "  +  c  +  "<br
/>");
c++;
}
document.write("Loop Terminates!");
//-->
</script>
```

<p>Change the values of the looping variable to see how things change</p>

</body>

</html>

The output of the code upon execution is shown in the image given below.

Do...While Loop

Another looping construct is the do...while loop. The condition's validity is checked at the end of the loop. So, this loop is that it executes at least once. This type of a loop executes the set of statements inside the do...while loop until the expression for the while is true. As soon as the expression becomes false, the while loop execution terminates. The syntax for implementation of while is given below –

do{

//Statements of the while block

}while (expression)

Sample implementation of the do...while loop is given below –

<html>

<body>

<script type="text/javascript">

<!--

var c = 0;

document.write("Loop begins...");

do{

document.write("Value of c: " + c + "<br />");

c++;

} while (c < 5)

document.write("Loop Terminates!");

//-->

</script>

<p>Change the values of the looping variable to see how things change</p>

</body>

</html>

The output of the code upon execution is shown in the image given below.

For Loop

The most commonly used looping construct is the 'for' loop. The for loop integrates the looping variable initialization, condition checking and looping variable update in the for statement. The syntax for implementation of while is given below –

for(init; expression; update){

//Statements of the for block

}

Here, init is the initialization statement and expression is the condition, which is to be tested. Lastly, the update is the expression that updates the looping variable. Sample implementation of the while loop is given below –

<html>

<body>

<script type="text/javascript">

```
<!--

var c;

document.write("Loop begins...");

for(c=0; c<5; c++){

document.write("Value of c: " + c + "<br
/>");

}

document.write("Loop Terminates!");

//-->

</script>
```

<p>Change the values of the looping variable to see how things change</p>

</body>

</html>

The output of the code upon execution is shown in the image given below.

For...In Loop

This loop is typically used with objects. The loop uses a variable of the object and loops through until the value of the property associated with the object variable is exhausted. In other words, this loop works around object properties. The syntax for the implementation of the for...in loop is as follows –

```
for (variable in object){

//Statements inside the for...in loop block

}
```

Sample implementation to demonstrate the working of the for...in loop is given below.

```
<html>

<body>

<script type="text/javascript">

<!--

var demoObject;

document.write("Properties of the Object: <br />
");

for (demoObject in navigation) {

document.write(demoObject);

document.write("<br />");

}

document.write ("Loop Terminated!");

//-->

</script>

<p>Change the object to see how the result changes</p>

</body>
```

```
</html>
```

Controlling the Loop

Although, once the loop starts, it terminates only when the expression stated for condition holds false, there are certain ways in which the developer can control the loop. There may be situation where you might want to terminate the loop in between execution if a special case occurs or you may want to start a new iteration on the occurrence of a scenario. In order to control and implement all these conditions, JavaScript has provided continue and break statements.

Break Statement

Whenever this keyword is encountered in a JavaScript code, the loop immediately terminates and execution is shifted to the statement that comes right after the closing bracket of the loop. In order to understand the working of break statement, let us take an example,

```
<html>
<body>
 <script type="text/javascript">
<!--
var a = 5;
```

```
document.write("Loop          Begins...<br        />
");

while (a < 30)        {

if (a == 5){

break;

}

a = a + 1;

document.write( a + "<br />");

}

document.write("Loop terminates!<br /> ");

//-->

</script>
```

<p>Change the value of a to see how the loop execution is modified</p>

```
</body>

</html>
```

The output of the code is shown in the image given below.

Continue Statement

When this statement is encountered in a loop, the rest of the loop statements are ignored and the control is shifted to the next iteration of the loop.

With that said, it is important to understand that the next iteration is execution only if the loop condition is found true. In case, the loop expression is found false, loop execution is terminated.

The sample code given below demonstrates the use of continue statement.

```
<html>

<body>

<script type="text/javascript">

<!--

var a = 0;

document.write("Loop          begins<br          />
");

while (a < 9){

a = a + 1;

if (a == 4){

continue; // skip rest of the loop body

}

document.write( a + "<br />");

}

document.write("Loop terminates!<br /> ");

//-->
```

```
</script>
```

<p>Change the value of a to see how the result changes!</p>

```
</body>
```

```
</html>
```

The output generated after execution of this code is illustrated in the image shown below.

Labels for Controlling Loop Flow

While the break and continue statements can redirect flow of control around the boundaries of the loop construct, they cannot be used to transfer control to precise statements. This is made possible in JavaScript with the use of labels. A label is simply an identifier followed by colon, which is placed before the statement or code block. The following code demonstrates the use of labels.

```
<html>
```

```
<body>
```

```
<script type="text/javascript">
```

```
<!--
```

```
document.write("Loop begins!<br /> ");
```

```
loop1: for (var i = 0; i < 3; i++) {
```

```
document.write("Loop1:    "   +   i   +    "<br
/>");
```

```
loop2: for (var j = 0; j < 3; j++) {

if (j > 3 ) break ; // Quit the innermost
loop

if (i == 2) break loop1; // Do the same
thing

if (i == 4) break loop2; // Quit the outer
loop

document.write("Loop2: " + j + " <br
/>");

}

}

document.write("Loop terminates!<br /> ");

//-->

</script>

</body>

</html>
```

The output of the code has been illustrated in the image given below.

Chapter 4. An Introduction to ES6

Some of the key features of ES6 are:

Arrows - Arrows is a function shorthand using the '=>' syntax. It is syntactically similar to the related feature in C#, Java 8 and CoffeeScript.

Classes - There is support for classes, inheritance, super calls, instances and static methods.

Template strings - Template strings are used for constructing strings.

Modules - There is language-level support for component definition modules.

Data structures - There is support for Maps, Sets, WeakMaps and WeakSets.

Most modern browsers have support for ES6. If you want to try out ES6 code, there are a few online editors that can help you do so. Below are two of my favourites. Both of them provide the next generation of JavaScript compilers.

https://jsbin.com

https://babeljs.io/

Let's now look at some simple examples of ES6 JavaScript code. In these examples we are going to use JS Bin to enter and run the code.

Example 55: The following program is a simple example of ES6 scripting.

```
let num1=5;

        console.log(num1);
```

The following should be noted about the above program:

The 'let' command is used to assign values to variables.

We then output the value of the variable using the 'console.log' command.

With this program, the output is as follows:

5

We can also declare constants using the 'const' keyword. Let's look at an example of this.

Example 56: The next program is an example of ES6 scripting using constants.

```
const num=6;

let num1=5;
```

```
console.log(num);
console.log(num1);
```

With this program, the output is as follows:

6

5

We can also define functions in ES6. Let's look at a simple example.

Example 57: The program below is an example of ES6 scripting using functions.

```
var start=function()
        {
const num=6;

let num1=5;

        console.log(num);
        console.log(num1);
        }
        start();
```

With this program, the output is as follows:

6

5

Decision Making and Loops

ES6 has support for the following Decision Making and Loop commands.

If statement - This is used to evaluate an expression and then execute statements accordingly.

If...else statement - This is used to evaluate an expression and then execute statements accordingly. Then execute another set of statements if the Boolean expression evaluates to false.

Nested if statements - This is useful to test multiple conditions.

Switch...case statement - This evaluates an expression, matches the expression's value to a case clause, and executes the statements associated with that case.

For loop - Here a set of statements are executed 'n' number of times.

While loop - Here a set of statements are executed until a condition remains true.

Do...while loop - Here a set of statements are executed until a condition remains true. The difference from the while loop is that one execution of the statements will always occur.

Let's look at some examples of these statements.

Example 58: The following program is an example of loops (if else) in ES6.

```
var start=function()

        {
const num=6;

let num1=5;

 if(num<7){

console.log("The value is less than 7");}

 else{

console.log("The value is greater than 7");

 }

        }
        start();
```

With this program, the output is as follows:

"The value is less than 7"

Example 59: The next program is an example of loops (for loop) in ES6.

```
var start=function()

        {
 for(x=0;x<5;x++)

  {
```

```
    console.log(x);

}

    }
    start();
```

With this program, the output is as follows:

0

1

2

3

4

<u>Example 60: This program is an example of loops (while loop) in ES6.</u>

```
var start=function()

        {
  let x=0;

  while(x<5)

    {

      console.log(x);

      x++;
```

```
    }
  }
  start();
```

With this program, the output is as follows:

0

1

2

3

4

Classes

ES6 also has the support for classes. A class can be defined as follows:

```
class classname
  {
  constructor(parameters)
  {
//Assign values to the properties

  }
// More methods

  }
```

Where:

'classname' is the name assigned to the class.

We have a constructor that is called when an object is created.

The constructor can take in parameters. These parameters can be used to assign values to the properties of the class.

We can then have more methods defined in the class.

Let's look at an example of a simple class in ES6.

Example 61: The following program shows how to use classes in ES6.

```
var start=function()

        {
  class Rectangle

    {

        constructor(height, width) {

      this.height = height;

      this.width = width;

    }

        Display()

        {
```

```
    console.log(this.height);

    console.log(this.width);

  }

 }

var newrect=new Rectangle(3,4);

newrect.Display();

    }
    start();
```

The following things can be noted about the above program:

First we define a class called 'Rectangle'.

It accepts 2 parameters, namely 'height' and 'width'.

This can be used to define the properties of 'height' and 'width' for the class.

We then create a 'Display' method that can be used to display the properties of the class.

With this program, the output is as follows:

3

4

Collections

ES6 also has the support for collections, such as the map collection. As an example, if we want to set the value of a map collection, we would use the 'set' method as shown below:

mapname.set(key,value);

Where:

- 'mapname' is the name of the map.
- 'key' is the key assigned to the element.
- 'value' is the value associated with that key.

Let's look at an example of using maps with ES6.

Example 62: The program below shows how to use maps in ES6.

```
var start=function()
        {
  var map = new Map();

  map.set('keyA','valueA');

  map.set('keyB','valueB');

  map.set('keyC','valueC');

  console.log(map.get("keyB"));
```

```
        }
    start();
```

With this program, the output is as follows:

valueB

Chapter 5.   Form

Form takes information from the web page visitors and sends it to a back-end application such as PHP script, CGI or ASP Script. HTML forms are used to collect data from visitors on a site. Forms are important for membership registration on a website, online shopping, or a job application form. For instance, during user registration, information such as email address, name, credit card, and so on would be collected. Then required processing would be performed on the sent data based on the specific logic contained in the back-end application. There are different available form elements such as the text area fields, radio buttons, drop-down menus, checkboxes, etc.

Form structure

<form>

HTML form is created with the <form> element. This tag must carry the action attribute at all times and would occasionally have an id and method attribute too.

Action

An action attribute is required for every <form> element. The value of the action attribute is the URL it contains for the page on the server which retrieves the information contained in the submitted form.

Method

Forms go to the back-end application in two ways. They "get" or "post".

Get

The GET method enables value from the form to return to the end of the specified URL in the action attribute. The GET method is perfect for data collection from the web server. The technique ensures parameter stores in the browser cache. There are limits of the quantity of information this method can send. Do not use the GET method while dealing with sensitive information such as passwords or credit card numbers because of the process that displays in the browser's address bar is visible to everyone.

Post

The POST method sends values through the HTTP headers. The POST method is perfect when the form contains sensitive information such as passwords and when visitors need to upload files. Parameters do not get saved in web server cache or browser history. The POST method is safer than the GET method.

Id

This value specifies a unique identity for an HTML form from other elements on the page.

Text input

The <input> tag enables the creation of different form controls. The type of attribute value determines the type of input created.

type="text"

With the type attribute value of the text, it creates a single line of text.

Name

When information is entered into a form by the user, the server demands to know what value the control data holds. For instance, in a login form, the server wants to know which declares the username and the password. Each form control needs the name attribute, and the attribute value recognizes the form control which is sent together with the information entered into the server.

Max length

The max length attribute can be used to determine the number of characters entered into a text field. The value of the max length attribute is the number of characters that it holds.

Password input

type="password"

The <input> tag of type "password" creates a way for users to input a password safely. The element presents a one-line plain text editor control replacing characters with a symbol such as the ("*") or a dot (" • ") which cannot be read and keeps the text secured.

Name

This attribute specifies the name of the password input which is transferred to the server including the password visitors enter.

<body>

<form action="http://www.alabiansolutions.com/login.php">

<p>Username:

<input type="text" name="username" size="15"maxlength="30" />

</p>

<p>Password:

<input type="password" name="password" size="15"maxlength="30" />

</p>

</form>

</body>

Textarea

A multi-line input is created with the <textarea> element. The <textarea> is not an empty element compared to other input elements, therefore, it should contain an opening and closing tag. Texts that surface between the opening <textarea> and closing </textarea> elements will be displayed in the text box when the page is loaded.

<form action="process.php">

<p>What did you think of this gig? </p>

<textarea name="comment"></textarea>

</form>

Radio Button

The <input type="radio"> element represents a radio button. It is used to create several selectable options.

Name

To be treated as a group, the value of the name attribute must correspond with the radio group because selecting any other radio button in the same group deselects the first selected button. A lot of radio groups can be created on a page as long as each has its name.

Value

The value attribute indicates the unique value connected with each selected option. Values of each button in a group should be different so the server can recognise the selected option.

Checked

The checked attribute specifies the selected value when the page loads. This attribute should be used by one radio button in a group.

<body>

Pizza Size:

<label>

<input type="radio" name="size" value="small"/>Small</label>

<label>

<input type="radio" name="size" value="medium"/>Medium

</label>

<label>

<input type="radio" name="size" value="large"/>Large

</label>

</body>

Checkbox

Checkbox is used to select and deselect one or more options.

type="checkbox"

Users are permitted to select or deselect one or more options in response to a question.

Name

This attribute is transferred to the server alongside the value of the option(s) selected by the user. The name attribute value must remain the same for all buttons when users have to respond to questions with options for answers in the checkboxes form.

Value

When a checkbox is checked, this attribute specifies the value sent to the server.

Checked

The checked attribute specifies the box that should be checked when the page is being loaded.

<body>

Pizza Toppings:

<label>

<input type="checkbox" value="bacon" />Bacon

</label>

<label>

<input type="checkbox" value="extra cheese" />Extra Cheese

</label>

```
<label>

<input type="checkbox" value="extra cheese"
/>Onion

</label>

</body>
```

Dropdown list box

A select Box, also known as the Drop-down list box enables the user to choose one option from a drop-down list. A drop-down list box is created with the <select> tag, and it consists of two or more <option> tags.

Name

The name attribute shows the form control name, which is being sent to the server together with the value selected by the user.

<option>

This element is used to indicate the options for a visitor. The text in-between the opening <option> and closing </option> elements will be displayed to the visitor in a drop-down box.

Value

The <option> tag utilises the value attribute to specify the value sent to the server together with the control name when the option is selected.

Selected

This attribute is used to specify the option that should be automatically selected when the page loads.

```
<body>

<label>Phones:

<select name="devices">

      <option value="techno">Sony</option>

  <option value="infinix">Infinix</option>

                              <option value="samsung">Samsung</option>

      <option value="sony" selected>Choose a device</option>

</select>

</label>

</body>
```

File input box

The file input box is used to enable users to upload a file on a web page. A file could be an image, audio, PDF or video.

type="file"

This input produces a box, a text input lookalike accompanied with a browse button. When the browse button is selected, a window pops up which enables users to select a file from their computer in order to be uploaded on the site.

```
<form action=" process.php" method="post">

<p>Upload your songs in MP3 format:</p>

<input type="file" name="user-song" /><br />

<input type="submit" value="Upload" />

</form>
```

type="submit"

This attribute is used when a user needs to submit a form.

```
<body>

<form action="process.php" method="post">

<p>Subscribe to our email list:</p>

<input type="text" name="email" value="email" />

<input type="submit" value="subscribe" />

</form>

</body>
```

Name

It can use a name attribute although it's not necessary.

Value

The value attribute is used to influence the appearance of the text on a button. It is advisable to designate the words that appear on a button because buttons default value on some browsers is "Submit query" and this can be inappropriate for forms.

Reset button

type="reset"

This button is used to erase all inputs by the user.

<input type="reset" value="Reset" />

Image button

An image can be used for the submit button. The type attribute must be given the value of the image. The SRC attribute can also be provided

<form action="http://www.websitename.com/subscribe.php">

<p>Subscribe to our email list:</p>

<input type="text" name="email" />

<input type="image" src="subscribe.png" width="100" height="20"

alt="Subscribe" />

</form>

Button Tag

The <button> tag specifies a button that can be clicked. Texts, content, or images can be inserted into the <button> element. The buttons created with the <input> element is different from buttons created with the <button> tag. The <button> element attribute type should always be specified.

<button type="submit">Click Me! </button>

Fieldset Element

Longer forms benefit a lot from the <fieldset> element. It is used to group form controls that are related together.

<form method="post">

<fieldset>

<legend>Contact Details</legend>

<label>Address:

<input type="text" name="text">

</label>

<label>Phone Number:

<input type="number" name="number">

</label>

<label>Email:

<input type="email" name="email">

```
      </label>

</fieldset>

</form>
```

Legend element

The <legend> element appears immediately after the opening <fieldset> tag and consists of a caption which identifies the motive of that form control group.

```
<form method="post">

 <fieldset>

<legend>Contact Details</legend>

<label>Address:<br>

<input type="text" name="text"><br>

</label>

<label>Phone Number:<br>

<input type="number" name="number"><br>

</label>

<label>Email:<br>

                    <input            type="email"
name="email"><br>

</label>

 </fieldset>
```

```
</form>
```

Label element

The label tag can be used to caption a form control so that users would know what should be entered into the area.

```
<form >
      <label for="male">Male</label>
<input type="radio" name="gender" id="male" value="male"><br>
      <label for="female">Female</label>
 <input type="radio" name="gender" id="female" value="female"><br>
      <label for="other">Other</label>
 <input type="radio" name="gender" id="other" value="other"><br><br>
 <input type="submit" value="Submit">
</form>
```

Chapter 6. Iframe and Multimedia

Iframe

The <iframe> element can be used to embed web pages into your web page.

Iframe embeds: Google Map

Google map can be embedded into your webpage using the iframe tag.

<iframe

src="https://www.google.com/maps/embed?pb=!1 m18!1m12!1m3!1d3963.341775346873!

2d3.34222531148425853!3d6.604381995223933!2 m3!1f0!2f0!3f0!3m2!1i1024!2i768!4f1

3.1!3m3!1m2!1s0x103b8d7c33eb87b3%3A0xfc23c 9556f669273!2sWebsite+Name!5e0!3m2!1sen!2sn g!4v1516009132030" width="600" height="450"

frameborder="0"   style="border:0" allowfullscreen></iframe>

Iframe embeds: YouTube

<body>

<iframe width="450" height="400"

src="https://www.youtube.com/embed/MhPGaOTi K0A"

frameborder="0" allowfullscreen></iframe>

</body>

Multimedia in HTML5

HTML5 enables users to embed video or audio using the native HTML tags. The browser will give users control to play the file if it supports it. Both audio and video tags are new features and can be used on the recent version of browsers. Popular video formats are .mp4, .m4v, Flash Video {.flv}, Audio Video Interleave {.avi} etc.

The video element:

A video player can be embedded using the video element for a specific video file. Those attributes are used to customize the player: preload, loop, auto play, poster, auto and controls.

Preload

The preload attribute instructs the browser on what action to take when the page loads. one of these three values can occur:

None: The video should not load automatically when the page loads until the user clicks play.

Auto: when the page loads the browser should download the video.

Metadata: this means that information such as first frame, size, track list and duration should be received by the browser.

Src

The path to the video is specified by this attribute.

Poster

This attribute enables users to direct an image to be displayed while the video downloads or until the user decides to play the video.

Width, height

The size of the player is specified with these attributes.

Controls

This attribute specifies that the browser should provide its own controls for playback when used.

Autoplay

This attribute indicates that the file should play automatically when used.

Loop

This attribute specifies that the video should start playing again from the beginning the moment it ends when utilized.

Multiple video formats

HTML5 enables users state multiple sources for audio and video elements so that browsers can use any one that works for them.

```html
<video     poster="images/calvin.jpg"     controls
preload="none" width="450" height="420">

<source src="calvin.mp4" type="video/mp4" />

<source src="calvin.webm" type="video/webm" />

<source src="calvin.ogv" type="video/ogv" />

<p>Calvin Harris music video</p>

</video>
```

The audio element

Embedding an audio player into a page for a particular audio file is done using the audio element. Different attributes can be used to customize the player, attributes such as auto play, controls, loop and preload.

Autoplay

This is a boolean attribute. If utilized, the audio will play automatically and continue without stopping.

Loop

The loop attribute is also a boolean attribute, and it states that the audio will restart over and over again every time the audio ends.

```html
<body>

<audio      src="avicii.mp3"      controls="true"
autobuffer="true"></audio>

</body>
```

Control

Audio controls are inserted using the control attribute, and it includes controls like pause, play, and volume. The <source> element enables the user to indicate alternative audio files that the browser could choose from. The browser would recognize the first organized format. Texts between the <audio> and </audio> elements will be displayed in browsers that do not recognize the <audio> element.

<audio   src="audio/test-audio.ogg"   controls autoplay>

      <p>This browser does not support our audio format. </p>

</audio>

Multiple audio formats

<audio controls autoplay>

<source src="audio/test-audio.ogg" />

<source src="audio/test-audio.mp3" />

<p>This browser does not support our audio format. </p>

</audio>

Chapter 7. The Document Object Model

The document object refers to your whole HTML page. After you load an object into the web browser, it immediately becomes a document object, which is the root element representing the html document. It comes with both properties and methods. The document object helps us add content to the web pages.

It is an object of the window, which means that having:

window.document

Is the same as having?

document

DOM Methods

DOM methods are the actions that you can perform on the html elements. The **DOM** properties are the values of the **HTML** elements which one can set or change. The following are the document object methods:

1. write("string")- it writes a string to a document.

2. writeln("string")- it writes a string to a document with a new line character.
3. getElementById()- gives the element with the specified id.
4. getElementsByName()-gives all the elements with the specified name.
5. getElementsByTagName()-gives all the elements with the specified tag name.
6. getElementsByClassName()-gives all the elements with the specified class name.

Accessing Field Values

The DOM is a good way of getting the values of an input field. Many are the times you will need to get input from a user. This can be done using the following property:

document.formname.name.value

Where:

- document- is the html document representing our root element.
- form name- is the name of the form with the fields.
- field name- is the name of the input text.
- value- is a property which returns the value of input text.

Consider the following example:

<html>

```
<body>
<script type="text/javascript">
    function readValue(){
                                        var
name=document.memberform.memberName.value;
    alert("Hi: "+name);
    }
    </script>
    <form name="memberform">
        Enter     Name:<input      type="text"
name="memberName"/>
        <input   type="button"   onclick="readValue()"
value="Click Here"/>
    </form>
</body>
</html>
```

When you run the code, it will give you the following simple form:

Just enter your name in the input field and click the Click Here button. See what happens.

You will get an alert box with your name and some text appended to it:

We simply created a simple form with an input text field. The method READVALUE() helps us get the value that we enter into the field. Consider the following line:

var name=document.memberform.memberName.value;

The MEMBERNAME is the name given to the text field in the form, and these must match, otherwise, you will not the right results.

getElementById()

Other than the name, we can also get the element by its id. This can be done using the DOCUMENT.GETELEMENTBYID() method. However, the input text field should be given an id.

 For example:

```
<html>

<body>

<script type="text/javascript">

    function computeSquare(){

    var x=document.getElementById("integer").value;

    alert(x * x);

    }

    </script>
```

```
<form>
```

Enter an Integer:`<input type="text" id="integer" name="myNumber"/><br/>`

`<input type="button" value="Compute Square" onclick="computeSquare()"/>`

```
</form>
```

`</body>`

`</html>`

The code should give you the following simple form upon execution:

Enter a number in the input field and click the Compute Square button.

This should return the square of the number in a popup box as shown below:

In the example, we have defined the COMPUTESQUARE() method which helps us get the square of a number entered in the input text field. Consider the following line:

var x=document.getElementById("integer").value;

In the line, we have used the GETELEMENTBYID() method which takes the id of the input text field as the argument. The method helps us get the value typed in the input text field using its id.

getElementsByName()

The DOCUMENT.GETELEMENTSBYNAME() method can help us get an element by its name. The method has the syntax given below:

document.getElementsByName(*"name"*)

The name is needed.

Example:

<html>

<body>

<script type=*"text/javascript"*>

   function getNumber()

   {

         var options=document.getElementsByName(*"option"*);

     alert("Total Options:"+*options.length*);

   }

   </script>

   <form>

     Yes:<input type=*"radio"* name=*"option"* value=*"yes"*>

     No:<input type=*"radio"* name=*"option"* value=*"no"*>

     <input type=*"button"* onclick=*"getNumber()"* value=*"Available Options"*>

```
</form>
```

```
</body>
```

```
</html>
```

Upon execution, the code returns the following:

Click the Available Options button and see what happens. A popup window will be shown as follows:

We have created two radio buttons with options YES and NO. Note that these two input types have been given the same name, that is, OPTION.

Consider the following line:

var options=^{document}.getElementsByName(*"option"*);

The line helps us count the number of elements with the name OPTION. This should be **2** as shown in the output.

getElementsByTagName()

The   DOCUMENT.GETELEMENTSBYTAGNAME() property returns the elements with the tag name which is specified. It takes the syntax given below:

^{document}.getElementsByTagName(*"name"*)

For example:

```
<html>
```

```
<body>
```

```
<script type="text/javascript">
function allparagraphs(){
var pgs=document.getElementsByTagName("p");
        alert("Total paragraphs are: "+pgs.length);
}
</script>
    <p>This is a paragraph</p>
    <p>This is a paragraph</p>
    <p>This is a paragraph</p>
    <p>This is a paragraph</p>
<button onclick="allparagraphs()">Total Paragraphs</button>
</body>
</html>
```

The code returns the following upon execution:

Click the Total Paragraphs button and see what happens.

You will see the following popup:

This means that the code was able to count the number of paragraphs that we have.

The main logic lies in the following line:

```
var pgs=document.getElementsByTagName("p");
```

We have passed the tag **"p"** as the argument to our method, and the tag represents a paragraph. There are three elements with the tag **"p"**, so the output should be **4** paragraphs.

Here is another example:

< html>

<body>

<script type=*"text/javascript"*>

function countheader2(){

var h2count=^{document}.getElementsByTagName(*"h2"*);

^{alert}("Total   count   for   h2   tags: "+*h2count.length*);

}

function countheader3(){

var h3count=^{document}.getElementsByTagName(*"h3"*);

^{alert}("Total   count   for   h3   tags: "+*h3count.length*);

}

</script>

<h2>A h2 tag</h2>

<h2>A h2 tag</h2>

<h2>A h2 tag</h2>

```
<h2>A h2 tag</h2>

<h3>A h3 tag</h3>

<h3>A h3 tag</h3>

<h3>A h3 tag</h3>

<h3>A h3 tag</h3>

<h3>A h3 tag</h3>

<button onclick="countheader2()">Total h2</button>

<button onclick="countheader3()">Total h3</button>

</body>

</html>
```

The code returns the following output upon execution:

We have a total of **4 h2** tags and a total of **5 h3** tags. Click the Total **h2** button and see what happens.

You should get the following popup box:

Click the Total **h3** button and see what happens.

You should get the following popup box:

innerHTML

This property can be used for addition of a dynamic content to an html page. It is used on html pages when there is a need to generate a dynamic content like comment form, registration form, etc.

Consider the following example:

```
<html>

<body>

<script type="text/javascript" >

function displayform() {

        var data="Username:<br><input
        type='text'
        name='name'><br>Comment:<br><texta
        rea                            rows='6'
        cols='45'></textarea><br><input
        type='submit' value='Contact us'>";
document.getElementById('area').innerHTML=data;

 }

</script>

<form name="form1">

<input    type="button"    value="Contact    us"
onclick="displayform()">

<div id="area"></div>

</form>

</body>

</html>
```

The code returns the following button upon execution:

Click the button and see what happens. You will get the following:

What we have done is that we are creating a contact us form after the user has clicked a button. Note that the html form has been generated within a div that we have created and given it the name AREA. To identify the position, we have called the DOCUMENT.GETELEMENTBYID() method.

innerText

We can use this property to add a dynamic property into an HTML page. Note that when this property is used, your text is interpreted as a normal text rather than as html content. A good application of this is when you need to write the strength of a password based on its length, write a validation message etc.

For example:

<html>

<body>

<script type="text/javascript" >

function validatePass() {

var message;

if(document.form1.userPass.value.length>5){

```
message="good";

}

else{

message="poor";

}

document.getElementById('area').innerText=message
;

 }
```

</script>

```
<form name="form1">

<input          type="password"          value=""
name="userPass" onkeyup="validatePass()">

Strength:<span   id="area">   Pasword   strength
</span>

</form>

</body>

</html>
```

The code returns the following upon execution:

Just begin to type the password and see what happens to the text on the right of the input field as you type. If you type less than 5 characters for the password, the message will change to poor as shown below:

Continue to type the password until you have more than 5 characters. You will see the message change to good as shown below:

That is how powerful this property is.

Animations

With JavaScript, we can animate elements. We can use JavaScript to move elements such as **<img />**, **<div>** etc. on a page depending on an equation. The following are the common methods used for animations in JavaScript:

1. setTimeout(method, time)- this method will call the METHOD after someTIME in milliseconds.
2. setInterval (method, time)- the method will call the METHOD after TIME milliseconds.

With JavaScript, one can set some attributes of the **DOM** object such its position on the screen. The position of the object can be set using TOP and LEFT attributes.

This is demonstrated below:

// Set the distance from the left edge of the screen.

object.style.left = distance measures in points or pixels;

or

<u>// Set the distance from the top edge of screen.</u>

object.style.top = distance measures in points or pixels;

Manual Animation

In the following example, we will be animating the image towards the right:

```html
<html>
<body>
<script type="text/javascript">
        var image = null;

          function init(){
        image = document.getElementById('myImage');

        image.style.position= 'relative';

        image.style.left = '0px';

        }
            function moveImage(){

        image.style.left = parseInt(image.style.left) + 10
+ 'px';

        }
        window.onload =init;

    </script>
```

```
    </head>

  <body>

  <form>

  <img id="myImage" src="house.jpg" />

  <p>Click the button to move the image</p>

<input    type="button"    value="Move    Image"
onclick="moveImage();" />

  </form>

</body>

</html>
```

You should use the correct name of your image in the following line:

```
<img id="myImage" src="house.jpg" />
```

In my case, I have a .jpg image named <u>HOUSE</u>. When I run the code, it returns the following:

Click the **"Move Image"** button. The image should move to the right with each click. This is shown below:

Consider the following line in the script:

```
image = document.getElementById('myImage');
```

We are getting the image using its **ID**, then it is assigned to the IMAGE variable. The INIT() method

297

helps us set the initial position of the image on the window. The method will be called when the window is being loaded. The MOVEIMAGE() function will move the image towards the right by **10 pixels** after every click. To move the image towards the left, the value should be set as negative. The animation, in this case, is manual as we have to click a button.

Automated Animation

To automate the process of animating an element, we can use the SETTIMEOUT() function provided by JavaScript.

Example:

```
<script type="text/javascript">
        var image = null;
        var animate ;
        function init(){
                image =
document.getElementById('myImage');
                image.style.position= 'relative';
                image.style.left = '0px';
        }
        function animateImage(){
```

```javascript
            image.style.left = parseInt(image.style.left) + 10
+ 'px';

            animate = setTimeout(animateImage,20);

        }
        function stopAnimation(){

            clearTimeout(animate);

            image.style.left = '0px';

        }
        window.onload =init;

    </script>
  </head>
  <body>
    <form>

        <img id="myImage" src="house.jpg " />

        <p>Click  the  Animate  button  to  launch
animation</p>

            <input   type="button"   value="Animate"
onclick="animateImage();" />

            <input    type="button"    value="Stop"
onclick="stopAnimation();" />

    </form>
```

The code returns the following upon execution:

Click the "Animate" button. The animation should start. When you click the Stop button, the animation will stop.

The ANIMATEIMAGE() method is calling the SETTIMEOUT method which sets the position of the image after every 20 milliseconds. This will result in the animation of the image. The STOPANIMATION() method helps in clearing the timer which is set by the SETTIMEOUT() method. The object, which is the image, is set back to its initial position.

Rollover

We can use a mouse image to rollover an image in JavaScript. Once you move the mouse over the image, it will change to another image.

Example:

<html>

<body>

<script type="text/javascript">

    if(document.images){

       var img1 = new Image();

       img1.src = "ps.jpg";

       var img2 = new Image();

       img2.src = "house.jpg";

    }

```
    </script>

  </head>

  <body>

    <p>Move mouse over to rollover</p>

<a                              href="#"
onMouseOver="document.img.src=img2.src;"

onMouseOut="document.img.src=img1.src;">

    <img name="img" src="nicsam.jpg" />

    </a>

</body>

</html>
```

We have used the IF statement to check whether the image exists or not. We have the used the IMAGE() constructor so as to preload some new object named IMG1. The same has also been done to preload the second image, IMG2. The SRC is given the name of the image stored externally. The # helps to disable the link so that a URL is not opened once it is clicked. The method ONMOUSEOVER is called once the mouse cursor is moved over the image. The ONMOUSEOUT method will be called once the mouse cursor is moved out of the image.

Chapter 8.   Clauses

GROUP BY clause

The GROUP BY clause gathers in all the rows that have data in the specified columns. It will also allow the aggregate functions we talked about earlier to be performed on the columns as well. The best way to explain this is with an example:

- SELECT column1,
- SUM(column2)
- FROM "list-of-tables"
- GROUP BY "column-list";

GROUP BY clause syntax:

Let's assume that you want to retrieve data on the maximum salaries paid for each separate department. Your statement would look like this:

- SELECT max(salary), dept.
- FROM employee
- GROUP BY dept;

This statement is going to show the highest salary in each unique department by name. In short, the name of the person in each department who earns the most will be displayed along with their salary and the department they work in.
HAVING clause

The HAVING clause is the one that lets you specify conditions on rows for each specific group, in other words, certain rows to be selected based on the specific conditions you input. The HAVING clause should always follow the GROUP BY clause if you are using it:

HAVING clause syntax:
- SELECT column1,
- SUM(column2)
- FROM "list-of-tables"
- GROUP BY "column-list"
- HAVING "condition";

The HAVING clause is best shown in an example so let's assume that you have a table that contains the names of your employees, the department they work in, their salary and their age. Let's say you want to find the average salary for each employee in each separate department, you would enter:

- # SELECT DEPT., AVG(SALARY)

  - **FROM employee**
  - **GROUP BY dept;**

But, let's now assume that you only want to calculate the average and display it if their salary is more than $20,000. Your statement would look like this:

- **SELECT DEPT, AVG(SALARY)**

  - **FROM employee**
  - **GROUP BY dept**

- **HAVING AVG(SALARY) > 20000;**

ORDER BY clause

The ORDER BY clause is optional and it lets you display your query results in an order that is sorted – either ascending or descending – based on whichever columns you choose to order the data by. *ORDER BY* clause syntax:

- SELECT column1, SUM(column2) FROM "list-of-tables" ORDER BY "column-list" [ASC | DESC];
- [ ] = optional

This statement is going to show the employee ID, department, their name, age and salary from the table you specify – in this case, the employee_info table – where the department is equal to SALES. The results will be listed in ascending order, sorted by salary:

- ASC = Ascending Order - default
- DESC = Descending Order
- For example:
- SELECT employee id, dept, name, age, salary FROM employee info WHERE dept = 'Sales' ORDER BY salary;

If you want to order data from multiple columns, each column name must be separated with a comma:

- SELECT employee_id, dept, name, age, salary
- FROM employee_info
- WHERE dept = 'Sales'
- ORDER BY salary, age DESC;

Chapter 9. Operators, Data Types and Other Priorities

JavaScript Calculations

All programming languages allow you to perform calculations. You can use JS, in a sense, as a replacement pocket calculator. For example, enter the following:

```
"use strict";

console.log(3 + 4);
```

Listing 5 accompanying_files/03/examples/c alc.js

As expected, you get *7* as your result.

You can see a few key JS concepts just in this very small, simple example. *3 + 4* is an EXPRESSION. Expressions are one of the most important concepts in JS. Expressions characteristically have a RETURN VALUE — in this case, the number *7*.

In turn, you can use return values in different places in your code, e. g. as an argument to a function call. Or to put this another way, JavaScript replaces expressions by their (return) values.

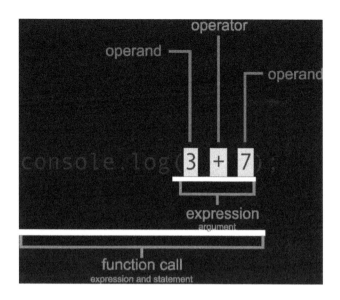

Expressions

Expressions in Firefox Web Console

You can also enter expressions directly into Firefox Web Console. Try entering *3 + 4* in the input line (next to the double arrow ") ().

Entering expressions directly in console — input

After you confirm your input with Return, the console will immediately display the return value ().

307

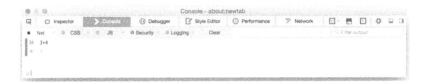

Entering expressions directly in console — output

FYI, you can also use Shift-Return to input a multi-line statement, i. e. a single statement which runs over multiple lines. The entire statement is executed only after you hit return.

Alternatively, you can also select parts of expressions in Scratchpad and examine these using **Inspect** (Ctrl-I / Cmd-I). As you see in , Scratchpad displays the result of *4 * 2* as *value: 8* in the side panel to the right.

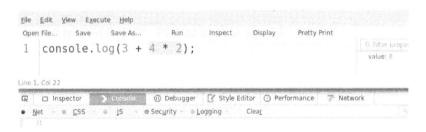

Inspect a selected (partial) expression in Scratchpad

Notation

From now on, we'll often point out a value returned by some expression or which appears at the console.

To do this, we'll insert a comment in the code and show the value in front of a => — the so-called FAT ARROW.

Example

```
3 + 4 // => 7

console.log(3 + 4 * 2); //=> 11
```

JavaScript as a Pocket Calculator: Arithmetic Operators

In addition to multiplication and addition operators, JS has corresponding operators for the arithmetic operations of **subtraction**, **division** and **modulus**. All of these operators fall under the group of so-called ARITHMETIC OPERATORS:

Symbol	Operation
+	Addition
-	Subtraction
*	Multiplication
/	Division

%	Modulus — remainder of an integer division
**	Exponentiation (ECMAScript 2016+)

Table *Arithmetic operators*

Example

2. *5 + 4* returns *9*

3. *5 - 4* returns *1*

4. *5 * 4* returns *20*

5. *5 / 4* returns *1.25*

6. *10 % 3* returns *1* since 10 - 3 * 3 = 1.

7. *5 ** 4* returns *625* since 5 * 5 * 5 * 5 = 625 .

Exercise 3: 2000 Seconds

How many minutes and remainder seconds are there in 2000 seconds? Use *console.log* to print out the answer.

Tips: The easiest way to solve this exercise is to use the modulus operator. Right now, we haven't taught you how to remove decimal places; we'll come back to that later.

Characters and Strings

Have you noticed anything about how numbers and text are coded differently? The *"Hello world"* at the beginning of the previous lesson was written out in quotation marks, while numbers were not. A text element is written out within quotation marks, and actually involves stringing or linking individual characters together — giving us the programming term STRING to indicate such text.

Two Types of Quotation Marks

You may use both single quotes or double quotes to delimit a string, but the marks at the beginning and at the end of the string must be the same.

Example

"Some text string" is allowed

'Some text string' is also allowed

"Some text string' is invalid

Most JS developers consistently use double quotes, and only use single quotes in exceptional cases, e. g. when they need to use double quotes within a string to indicate literal wording.

Coding Guidelines

You should normally use double quotes to delimit strings.

Determining Length

Sometimes you need to know how long a string is — i. e. how many characters are in it. As you do more and more development, you'll come across many situations where length is important.

For example, blogs, lists of products, and similar items sometimes provide a text preview which only shows part of the entire text. Before generating this preview, the length of the entire text item must first be measured to see whether the text actually needs to be shortened.

So at this point, we'd like to introduce you to the string property LENGTH. You can have a string return this property by typing **.length** after the string.

> "length matters - sometimes".length // => 26

Then pack your statement into a *console.log* so you can see the response you need on the console:

```
"use strict";

console.log("length matters -
sometimes".length);
```

***Listing 6* accompanying_files/03/examples/length.js**

Exercise 4: Lucky Numbers & Name Codes

Do you know about lucky numbers and code names? Here's an interesting way to come up with a name code:

> Multiply the length of your first name (including your middle name(s) if you want) by the length of your last name and print out the result in the console. (Just to let you know, these are the numbers we got: 40 and 30.)

Literals: They Say What They Mean

Now that you've been introduced to strings and numbers, there's another important concept we need to tell you about: Basically, any value — whether a string or a number — which is specified literally in your code is known as a (you guessed it) *literal*. Literals always have a fixed value.

Examples

    5. 42

    6. "house"

    7. "green"

    8. 5.47

    9. 1998

    10.   "Please enter your name"

Number & String Data Types

JavaScript literals have a so-called DATA TYPE. As the term implies, a data type specifies what kind of data the literal represents, and in turn its possible values.

Up to this point, we've used the following data types:

Data Type	Permissible Values / Meaning	Example of Literal
String	Any text	"Hello"
Number	Any positive or negative number	246.5

Table *String & number data types*

JavaScript encodes strings in so-called UTF-16 character format [ECMA-262]. An encoding format is responsible for how characters are represented digitally. UTF-16 makes it possible for you to use a wide variety of special characters as well as specific letters from different languages (e. g. German umlauts, accented French characters, etc.).

The value range for numbers is also limited. However, as long as you don't carry out any astronomical calculations, you should be safe.

It's easy to find out the data type of a literal — just use the JavaScript operator *typeof*. *typeof* returns a string which tells you the literal's data type.

Examples

    "use strict";

    console.log(typeof 3764);   // => number

    console.log(typeof "beautiful JS"); // => string

    console.log(typeof 27.31);   // => number

Listing 7 **accompanying_files/03/examples/type.js**

Exercise 5: Hmmm…So What are You Really?

    What is the data type of the following literal?

    "42"

Chapter 10. Document Object Model (DOM)

The document object is an object that is created by the browser for each new HTML page. When it is created, JavaScript allow us access to a number of properties and methods of this object that can affect the document in various ways, such as managing or changing information. As a matter of fact we have been continuously using a method of this object, document.write(), in order to display content in a web page. Nevertheless, before exploring properties and methods we will first take a look at the Document Object Model (DOM).

Fundamental DOM Concepts

We are aware that when the web browser receives an HTML file it displays it as a web page on the screen with all of the accompanying files like images and CSS styles. Nevertheless, the browser also creates a model of that web document based on its HTML structure. This means that all the tags, their attributes and the order in which they appear is remembered by the browser. This representation is called the Document Object Model (DOM) and it is used to provide information to JavaScript how to communicate with the web page elements.

Additionally, the DOM provides tools which can be used to navigate or modify the HTML code.

The Document Object Model is a standard defined by the World Wide Web Consortium (W3C) that is used by most browser developers. To better understand the DOM, let us first take a look at a very simple web page:

```
<!doctype html>

<html>

<head>

<meta charset="utf-8">

<title>Party Schedule</title>

<style type="text/css">

.current {

color:red;

}

.finished {

color:green;

}

</style>

</head>

<body>
```

```
<h1 id="partytitle">Party Plan</h1>

<ul id="partyplan">

  <li id="phase1">20:00 - Home warm-up</li>

  <li id="phase2">22:00 - Joe's Bar</li>

  <li id="phase3">00:00 - Nightclub 54</li>

</ul>

</body>

</html>
```

On a web page, tags wrap around other tags. The <html> tag wraps around the <head> and <body> tags. The <head> tag wraps around tags such as <title>, <meta> and <script>. The <body> wraps around all content tags such as <p>, <h1> through <h6>, <ul>, <table> and so on.

This relationship between tags can be represented with a tree structure where the <html> tag acts as the root of the tree, while other tags represent different tree branch structures dependent on the tag hierarchy within the document. In addition to tags, a web browser also memorizes the attributes of the tag as well as the textual content within the tag. In the DOM each of these items, tags, attributes and text, are treated as individual units which are called nodes.

Image 26. Tree structure of an HTML document

In the tree structure for our basic HTML page the <html> element acts as a root element, while the <head> and <body> elements are nodes. In defining this relationship we can also refer to <html> as the parent node, and the <head> and <body> elements as child notes. In turn, both the <head> and <body> elements contain child nodes and so on. When we reach an item that contains no other child node we terminate the tree structure at that node, also known as a leaf node.

Selecting Document Elements

With the DOM structure in place, JavaScript can access the elements within the document in several different ways, dependent on whether we want to select individual or multiple elements. In all approaches we first have to locate the node representing the element we need to access and subsequently use the content, child elements and attributes of that node.

Selecting Individual Elements

To select individual elements we most commonly use the getElementById() method. This method will let us select an element with a particular ID attribute applied to its HTML tag. This method is the most efficient way to access an element if we follow the presumption that the ID attribute is unique for every element within the page. In the following example we will access the element whose ID attribute has the value 'phase1':

var firststop = document.getElementById("phase1");

By using the getElementById() method on the document object means that we are searching for the element with this ID anywhere on the page. Once the 'phase1' element is assessed, which in our case is the first <h1> element, the reference to this node is stored in the firststop variable and we can use JavaScript to make changes. As an example we will assign the attribute class with the value 'current' to this element. We will include this code in a <script> tag in the <head> section of our document.

var firststop = document.getElementById("phase1");

firststop.className = "current";

Image 27. Changing the style of a page element

> *Note:* In some browsers we have to either put the <script> tag before the closing </body> tag or in an external .js file in order for the code in this chapter to work.

If we want to collect the text from a node, we can use the textContent property. More importantly, we can also use the textContent property to change the content of the node. In the following example we will first select the element that has the value 'partytitle' in its id attribute and assign it to the title variable. Then we will effectively change the text of this element by changing the textContent property of the title variable. Let us add the following lines to our JavaScript code:

var title = document.getElementById("partytitle");

title.textContent = "Party Schedule";

Image 28. Changing the content of a page element

Selecting Group Elements

While sometimes selecting an individual element will be sufficient, other times we may need to select a group of elements. For example, we might need to select all <li> tags on a page, or all elements that share a class attribute. In these cases JavaScript offers the following two methods:

- *getElementsByTagName()* – a method which will let us select every instance of a particular tag.
- *getElementsByClassName( )* – a method that retrieves all elements that share a particular class name.

Selecting a group of elements means that the method will return more than one node. This collection of nodes is known as a NodeList and will be stored in an array-like item. Each node will be given an index number, starting with 0, while the order of the nodes will be the same order in which they appear on the page. Although NodeLists look like arrays and behave like arrays, semantically they are a type of object called a collection. As an object, a collection has its own properties and methods which are rather useful when dealing with a NodeList.

The following example will select all <li> elements and assign their node references to the schedule variable.

```
var schedule =
document.getElementsByTagName("li");
```

If we want to access each element separately, we can use an array syntax. For example:

```
var item1 = schedule[0];
```

```
var item2 = schedule[1];
```

```
var item3 = schedule[2];
```

However, when we select a group of items we usually want to interact with the whole group. As an example, let us assign the class attribute with the "finished" value to all <li> elements. For this purpose we can use a loop to go through each element in the NodeList.

```
var schedule =
document.getElementsByTagName("li");
```

```
        for (var i = 0; i < schedule.length; i++) {
        schedule[i].className = "finished";
}
```

Image 29. Changing the class attribute for all <li> elements

Similarly to working with arrays, when working with collections we can use the length property to determine the size of the collection. We can then use this information in a for loop in order to effectively go through every NodeList item and assign the "finished" class attribute.

We can use exactly the same logic for the getElementsByClassName() method. We will get a NodeList stored in a collection with each node having an index number. Like with the getElementByTagName() method, we can access individual items and manage the collection through its object properties and methods.

Traveling Through the DOM

When we use any of the previously discussed methods to select an element node, we can also select other elements in relation to this elements. This type of relative selection is considered as an element property.

previousSibling & nextSibling

The previousSibling and nextSibling properties refer to adjacent elements on the same DOM level. For example, if we select the second <li> element with the id value "phase2", the "phase1" <li> element would be considered a previousSibling, while the "phase3" <li> element would be nextSibling. In the case where there is no sibling, (ex. the "phase1" element has no previousSibling), the value of this property remains null.

In the following example we select the <li> element which has "phase2" as a value for its id attribute and we change the class attribute for both the selected element and its previous sibling.

var secondstop = document.getElementById("phase2");

var prevstop=secondstop.previousSibling;

secondstop.className = "current";

prevstop.className = "finished";

Parents & Children

We can also travel to different levels of the DOM hierarchy using the selected element as a starting point. If we want to move one level up we can use the parentNode property. For example, if we have the second <li> element selected we can refer to its parent element, the <ul> element, with the following syntax:

var secondstop = document.getElementById("phase2");

var upperelement = secondstop.parentNode;

Alternatively, if we want to move one level down, we can use either the firstChild or the lastChild property. In the following example we have selected the <ul> element with "partyplan" as a value for its id attribute. Using the firstChild property we refer to the first <li> element of this list, while with the lastChild property we refer to the last <li> element of this list.

var plan = document.getElementById("partyplan");

var child1 = plan.firstChild;

var child2 = plan.lastChild;

Adding and Managing Content

Until this point we discussed how to find elements in the DOM. The more interesting aspect are the approaches to managing content within the DOM.

Changing HTML

We already talked about the textContent property, but this property retrieves only text values and ignores the subsequent HTML structure. If we want to edit the page HTML we have to use the innerHTML property. This property can be used on any element node and it is capable of both retrieving and editing content.

var liContent = document.getElementById("phase1").innerHTML;

When retrieving the HTML from the <li> element with "phase1" as a value for its id attribute, innerHTML captures the whole content of the element, text and markup, as a string variable. If we apply the same syntax for the <ul> element, the innerHTML property will capture all of the <li> items.

We can also use the innerHTML property to change the content of the element. If this content contains additional markup, these new elements will be processed and added to the DOM tree. For example, let us add the <em> tag to the first <li> item in the party list:

var firstStop = document.getElementById("phase1");

firstStop.innerHTML = "<em>20:00 - Home warm-up</em>";

Image 30. Adding an <em> element with content to the first list item

DOM Manipulation

A more direct technique to managing document content is to use DOM manipulation. This is a 3-step process that uses the following methods:

- *createElement()* - The process begins by creating a new element node with the createElement() method. This element node is stored in a variable and it is not yet a part of the DOM.

- *createTextNode()* - The process continues by creating a new text node with the createTextNode() method. Like in the previous step, this text node is stored in a variable and it is not a part of the document.
- *appendChild()* - The final step is adding the created element to the DOM tree with the appendChild() method. The element will be added as a child to an existing element. The same method can be used to add the text node to the element node.

As an example let us create a new element that we will add to the existing party list. We will use the createElement() method and add this element to the newPlan variable.

var newPlan = document.createElement("li");

Following, we will create a new text node and add its content as a value to the newPlanText variable.

var newPlanText =
document.createTextNode("04:00 - Back to home");

We can now assign the content of the text node to the newPlan element by using the appendChild() method.

newPlan.appendChild(newPlanText);

Finally, we would like to add this element to the list. We will use the getElementById() method to select the list through its "partyplan" id, and apply the appendChild() method to attach the newPlan element to the list.

document.getElementById("partyplan").appendChild(newPlan);

The complete syntax is as follows:

var newPlan = document.createElement("li");

var newPlanText =
document.createTextNode("04:00 - Back to home");
newPlan.appendChild(newPlanText);
document.getElementById("partyplan").appendChild(newPlan);
   Image 31. Adding a new <li> element

Using a similar process we can also use DOM manipulation to remove an element from the page. As an example let us remove the <h1> element which acts as the main page heading. We will first select the element through its id attribute with "partytitle" as its value and store that element node in a variable.

var removeHeading = document.getElementById("partytitle");

Next, we will need to find the parent element which acts as a container for the <h1> element, which in this case is the <body> element. We can either select this element directly, or use the parentNode property of the previously selected element. In either case we will need to store the parent element in another variable.

var containerForHeading = removeHeading.parendNode;

Finally, we will use the removeChild() method on the parent element in order to discard the element that we want removed from the page.

containerForHeading.removeChild(removeHeading);

The complete syntax is as follows:

var removeHeading = document.getElementById("partytitle");

var containerForHeading = removeHeading.parentNode;

containerForHeading.removeChild(removeHeading);

Image 32. Removed heading

Chapter 11. Events (Not the Kind You Celebrate)

If you can finish the new chat feature by tonight, we'll throw an office party to celebrate its release. Nothing fancy, just some drinks, good music and a little something to eat …

The chat code is now stored in a separate JavaScript file and is also a little cleaner. But Marty's not completely happy, there's still something missing...

Of course, visitors to the website shouldn't have to program JS to highlight chat members — highlighting should change automatically based on the input in the search box.

In order for that to happen, the code needs to react to user input. Your browser provides so-called EVENTS for just that purpose (no, we don't mean events like weddings or parties — unfortunately).

Browser Events

Any exertion of influence by a user, no matter how small, is considered by your browser to be an event. An event can be almost anything, including:

2) <u>clicking on a button</u>

3) <u>moving your mouse over an image</u>

4) releasing an input key

5) leaving an input field using your mouse or by tabbing

6) finger gestures on a touch screen, e. g. zoom

There're also events which aren't triggered directly by users, and are triggered instead through occurrences like network requests or files which have finished loading. But first, we'll concentrate only on those events directly related to user behavior.

Dealing With Events as They Come Up: Event Handlers

Preliminary Measures

First, try a small experiment in your console. The event you're interested in is a user releasing a key while typing in an input field. Look in the chat HTML document and you'll find the input field (INPUT element) within a DIV element with the ID *member_search*:

<div
id
member_search
<input
type
text

...Find a member...

/>

</div>

First, let's select the field using $('#MEMBER SEARCH INPUT'). You'll get back the INPUT element as a return value in the console. Move your cursor over the element in the console and you'll see that it's the right field.

Now, we'll bind an event to that field. To do this, we'll use the method ADDEVENTLISTENER. That method is available on almost every HTML element object.

$('#member search input').addEventListener(...);

ADDEVENTLISTENER requires two arguments. The first argument is the EVENT TYPE, in the form of a string. The event type we should use in this case is 'KEYUP', or releasing a key.

$('#member search input').addEventListener('keyup', ...);

ADDEVENTLISTENER's second argument must be a function — this will be executed by your browser when the specified event occurs. In this case, we'll just use a simple function to make sure the process is working:

() => alert(1)

FYI, the function you register on an event is called an EVENT LISTENER or EVENT HANDLER, and it's responsible for processing the event you specify.

And now our statement is complete — let's test it out in the console:

$('#member_search input').addEventListener('keyup', () => alert(1));

If you go to the member search input box and type in a character, an alert box with the alert 1 will appear as soon as you release the key. Of course, this function isn't very useful yet. And maybe clicking away alert boxes is making you a little irritated — but at least now you know how event handlers work. Mission accomplished!

Putting Everything Together

Now comes the tough part — you need to combine your existing code for highlighting and for event registration into one complete program.

Delete the call HIGHTLIGHTCHATMEMBERS('ERT'); from your JS file. Instead, your KEYUP event should now trigger the function call:

$('#member_search input')

  .addEventListener('keyup', () =>

```
    hightlightChatMembers('ert'));
```

And actually, as soon as you type a key in the search box, the highlighting changes. However, instead of permanently highlighting the string 'ERT', we want to use the actual input. But how can we do that?

Once again, we'll need to use the input element object. We can retrieve it by using the selector $('#MEMBER SEARCH INPUT'), then query it for the value input by the user. We'll find that value in the property VALUE, i. e. $('#MEMBER SEARCH INPUT').VALUE. You'll learn more about VALUE and other properties in **lesson 6**.

Putting it all together, we get the following statement:

```
$('#member search input')
   .addEventListener('keyup', () =>
    hightlightChatMembers($('#member search input').value));
```

Which then gives us the following overall code:

```
  1
"use strict";
  2
  3
```

```
4
  const          highlightChatMembersBy          =
partOfMemberName => {
5
   chatMembers()
6
     .filter(member =>
7
       doesMemberMatch(partOfMemberName,
member))
8
     .forEach(highlight);
9
 };
10
11
  const doesMemberMatch = (partOfMemberName,
memberElement) =>
12
   memberElement.innerHTML.toLowerCase()
13
     .includes(partOfMemberName.toLowerCase());
```

```
14

15

  const chatMembers = () => $$("#chat_members
li");

16

  const        highlight      =      el      =>
el.classList.add("highlighted");

17

18

  const                $                =
document.querySelector.bind(document);

19

  const                $$               =
document.querySelectorAll.bind(document);

20

  NodeList.prototype.  proto   = Array.prototype;

21

22

  $("#member_search input")

23

    .addEventListener("keyup", () =>

24
```

```
       highlightChatMembersBy($("#member_search
input").value));
```

25

Listing 16 accompanying_files/05/examples/highlig
ht_chat_members_1_event/highlight_chat_membe
rs.js

Enter different strings and experiment a little with
your current implementation. What do you notice?

Guard Clauses: Protection for Your Functions

*Oops — I just found a bug. If I search for a chat
member, suddenly* all *of them are highlighted.*

*Could you fix that? As it is, we can't possibly put the
highlight feature online.*

Okay, here's the problem — although the program
is highlighting the matching members, it's not
removing that highlighting again when the search
string is updated.

Instead of going through the trouble to find out what
highlighting we need to remove, it'd be a lot simpler
just to remove all highlighting, then highlight only
those chat members who match the search. To do
this, we'll need some additional code which removes
the corresponding CSS class from all members:

```
const removeHighlightsFromAllChatMembers = ()
=>
```

```
  chatMembers().forEach(removeHighlight);
```

```
const     removeHighlight     =     el     =>
el.classList.remove('highlighted');
```

FYI, it's not a problem that a few LI elements with chat members don't have the class *highlighted* at all — in that case, nothing will be removed.

Order the two functions according to their level of detail. In addition, we still need to add a call to the new function REMOVEHIGHLIGHTSFROMALLCHATMEMBERS. To do this, we recommend you create a higher-level function called UPDATEHIGHLIGHTINGOFCHATMEMBERS, which first removes all highlights (REMOVEHIGHLIGHTSFROMALLCHATMEMBERS) then marks the matching chat members (HIGHTLIGHTCHATMEMBERSBY):

```
const     updateHighlightingOfChatMembers     =
partOfMemberName => {

  removeHighlightsFromAllChatMembers();

  hightlightChatMembersBy(partOfMemberName);

};
```

Now we just need to add the new function UPDATEHIGHLIGHTINGOFCHATMEMBERS to the event handler in place of the function HIGHTLIGHTCHATMEMBERSBY, which was only responsible for highlighting. We then get the following code:

```
1
"use strict";

2

3

4
const updateHighlightingOfChatMembers =
partOfMemberName => {

5
  removeHighlightsFromAllChatMembers();

6
  highlightChatMembersBy(partOfMemberName);

7
};

8

9
const removeHighlightsFromAllChatMembers = ()
=>

10
  chatMembers().forEach(removeHighlight);

11
```

```
12  const        highlightChatMembersBy        =
    partOfMemberName => {
13    chatMembers()
14      .filter(member =>
15        doesMemberMatch(partOfMemberName,
    member))
16      .forEach(highlight);
17  };
18
19  const doesMemberMatch = (partOfMemberName,
    memberElement) =>
20    memberElement.innerHTML.toLowerCase()
21      .includes(partOfMemberName.toLowerCase());
```

```
22

23

  const chatMembers = () => $$("#chat_members
li");

24

  const        highlight        =        el        =>
el.classList.add("highlighted");

25

  const      removeHighlight      =      el      =>
el.classList.remove("highlighted");

26

27

  const                    $                    =
document.querySelector.bind(document);

28

  const                    $$                    =
document.querySelectorAll.bind(document);

29

  NodeList.prototype.  proto   = Array.prototype;

30

31

  $("#member_search input")
```

32

```
    .addEventListener("keyup", () =>
```

33

```
updateHighlightingOfChatMembers($("#member_s
earch_input").value));
```

34

Listing 17 accompanying_files/05/examples/highlig
ht_chat_members_2_remove/highlight_chat_mem
bers.js

The code from **listing 17** works … almost. It works
except for the small glitch that all members are
selected in case of blank input. But the empty string
occurs in every string!

We can suppress this behavior just by adding code
at   the   beginning   of   the   function
HIGHTLIGHTCHATMEMBERSBY to check whether
PARTOFMEMBERNAME is empty. In case of an empty
string, the function just needs to refuse to work. Add
a RETURN to make the function exit prematurely.

if (partOfMemberName === "") return;

Code like this, which runs before the main body of a
function is actually executed to make sure the
values of the arguments passed to the function
make   sense,   are   called   guard   clausesor   just

GUARDS. They protect functions from invalid input values.

```
const          hightlightChatMembersBy          =
partOfMemberName => {
  if (partOfMemberName === "") return;
  chatMembers()
    .filter(member                              =>
doesMemberMatch(partOfMemberName, member))
    .forEach(highlight);
};
```

Listing 18 The function highlightChatMembersBy with a guard

The code from **listing 18** finally behaves like it should. But before you run to Marty to bring him the good news, let's take a little time to add a couple of improvements. Your maintenance programmer will thank you for that someday!

Making a Stunning Entrance Using init

The event registration code is still just kind of out there, with no motivation — it would be better to put it into its own function. This will give us a number of advantages — the code will be reusable and it'll also have its own name, making it easier to identify. In addition, putting the code into a separate function will provide us advantages in terms of things we haven't yet covered in this class — e. g. the code will be easier to test.

A good function name might be *registerEvents*, or even just *init*. If we wanted to, we could get even more specific and name the function *registerEventsForChatMemberHighlighting*.
However, given the context (i. e. our entire file is geared for a specific task) the generic *init* is perfectly acceptable.

The name *init* stands for initialization. It's a function which calls all other functions, acting as an entry point into the rest of the code in the program. We could essentially name the function anything we wanted to, but *init* has already been established as the name for such functions. Other programmers can read the function name and understand immediately what we mean by it.

Based on our newspaper metaphor, INIT's function definition belongs at the beginning of your code. However, the call to INIT() can be made only after all other function have been defined.

```
1
"use strict";
2
3
4
```

```
  const init = () => $("#member_search input")
5
   .addEventListener("keyup", () =>
6

updateHighlightingOfChatMembers($("#member_s
earch input").value));
7
8
  const    updateHighlightingOfChatMembers    =
partOfMemberName => {
9
   removeHighlightsFromAllChatMembers();
10
   hightlightChatMembersBy(partOfMemberName);
11
  };
12
13
  const removeHighlightsFromAllChatMembers = ()
=>
14
```

```
   chatMembers().forEach(removeHighlight);
15
16
  const         hightlightChatMembersBy         =
partOfMemberName => {
17
   if (partOfMemberName === "") return;
18
   chatMembers()
19
    .filter(member =>
20
      doesMemberMatch(partOfMemberName,
member))
21
    .forEach(highlight);
22
 };
23
24
  const doesMemberMatch = (partOfMemberName,
memberElement) =>
```

```
25
    memberElement.innerHTML.toLowerCase()

26
      .includes(partOfMemberName.toLowerCase());

27

28
  const chatMembers = () => $$("#chat_members
li");

29
  const      highlight      =      el      =>
el.classList.add("highlighted");

30
  const      removeHighlight      =      el      =>
el.classList.remove("highlighted");

31

32
  const                    $                    =
document.querySelector.bind(document);

33
  const                    $$                    =
document.querySelectorAll.bind(document);

34
```

```
NodeList.prototype.  proto  = Array.prototype;
```

35

36

```
init();
```

37

Listing 19 accompanying_files/05/examples/highlig
ht_chat_members_3_init/highlight_chat_members.
js
Take a Look Behind the Facade With the Event
Object

The fact that our current code can use some
improvements will become clear once we take a
closer look at event registration.

```
$('#member search input')
  .addEventListener('keyup', () =>
    hightlightChatMembers($('#member search
input').value));
```

The function we'll register as our event handler here
is:

```
() => hightlightChatMembers($('#member search
input').value);
```

The interesting thing to note here is that the
function, when it's called by the event, is
automatically passed the event as an argument. So

we just need to implement a parameter to capture the event:

event => hightlightChatMembers($('#member_search input').value);

What can we do with the EVENT? One thing would be to print it out to the console to see what it contains:

event => {

  console.log(event);

  hightlightChatMembers($('#member_search input').value);

If you type the letter **a**, the console will show:

keyup { target: <input>, key: "a", charCode: 0, keyCode: 65 }

If you click on *keyup*, you'll see that EVENT is a JS object of "type"[1]KEYBOARDEVENT. Keyboard events have a number of very interesting properties — the table below shows you just a few:

1 In reality, JS doesn't have specific object types. It would be more correct to say that *keyup* is a JS object which has the KEYBOARDEVENT object in its prototype chain. We're using the term *type* here for purposes of simplification. It's only to show that all

objects of the same "type" also have the same properties.

Property	Content
type	keyup
code	KeyA
key	a
timeStamp	[timestamp, i. e. when the event occurred]
target	[element which triggered the event]
ctrlKey	false [was the Ctrl key pressed?]
altKey	false [was the Alt key pressed?]

Events have many other properties, but just the few we've listed above show you that an event object contains all the information which comes into play when an event occurs, e. g.:

- What type of event is it? *keyup*

- What key was released? *a*

- When was the event triggered?

- From where was the event triggered?

Your event handler can then put this information to use. TARGET is the property which is of primary interest to us in our current program. TARGET contains the input field we intend to use, which we'd otherwise select by using $('#MEMBER SEARCH INPUT'). Therefore, we could also register our event handler as follows:

event   =>
hightlightChatMembers(event.target.value);

Doing so gives us a number of concrete advantages. In all cases, it's more efficient, since your browser doesn't have to find the element object again — it's already in TARGET. But a much more important advantage is better maintainability. If our selector for finding the input field should change (e. g. because of a change to the HTML structure), we won't have to worry about also changing the event handler. It always refers to the current TARGET, no matter how we found the element and registered the event on it.

1

"use strict";

2

3

4

```
  const init = () => $("#member_search_input")
5
   .addEventListener("keyup", event =>
6

updateHighlightingOfChatMembers(event.target.val
ue));
7
8
  const     updateHighlightingOfChatMembers     =
partOfMemberName => {
9
   removeHighlightsFromAllChatMembers();
10
   hightlightChatMembersBy(partOfMemberName);
11
  };
12
13
  const removeHighlightsFromAllChatMembers = ()
=>
14
```

```
    chatMembers().forEach(removeHighlight);

15

16

  const          hightlightChatMembersBy          =
partOfMemberName => {

17

   if (partOfMemberName === "") return;

18

   chatMembers()

19

      .filter(member =>

20

        doesMemberMatch(partOfMemberName,
member))

21

      .forEach(highlight);

22

  };

23

24

  const doesMemberMatch = (partOfMemberName,
memberElement) =>
```

```
25
    memberElement.innerHTML.toLowerCase()
26
      .includes(partOfMemberName.toLowerCase());
27
28
  const chatMembers = () => $$("#chat members
li");
29
  const        highlight      =      el      =>
el.classList.add("highlighted");
30
  const      removeHighlight    =    el      =>
el.classList.remove("highlighted");
31
32
  const                    $                    =
document.querySelector.bind(document);
33
  const                  $$                  =
document.querySelectorAll.bind(document);
34
```

```
NodeList.prototype.__proto__ = Array.prototype;
```

35

36

```
init();
```

37

Listing 20 accompanying_files/05/examples/highlight_chat_members_4_target/highlight_chat_members.js

FYI, we can abbreviate EVENT as E. Normally abbreviations are considered "bad" and should be avoided, but in this case it's okay. The single letter E is a common abbreviation for EVENT and is acceptable as long as its scope (range over which a variable exists) is limited to a very small function.

Now we're ready! You can finally show Marty the improved feature, and he's so happy about it he throws another party — here's to hoping it'll be an unforgettable event!

Chapter 12. A Storing Information in Variables

Learning to use Variables

In this chapter we are going to discuss variables. Variables are important elements of any programming language, and Javascript is no exception.

Variables are memory allocations used to hold values. They are called variables because their value may vary over time throughout the execution of the program.

You can use variables to hold text values (also known as alphabetic or string values) such as a person's name, company name or any other text content in your program. Variables may also hold numerical values.

To show you how variables are used, let's start with an HTML document page. For this example, we will use an HTML 4.01 document. To insert Javascript, a script tag is used with attributes set as follows:

<script   language="javascript" type="text/javascript">

All Javascript commands must be placed within the script element. The first Javascript element that must be identified is the variable to be used. We need to name the variable and declare it.

When you declare a variable in Javascript, you use the *var* statement followed by the name of the variable. It is ideal that the name of the variable is something that describes what the variable represents. The variable name can be any alphanumeric set of characters, and should be treated as case sensitive. No punctuation marks or special characters are allowed, except for underscore.

An example of a variable declaration is:

var userName;

It's not required to use the var statement when declaring a variable in Javascript, however, it is a good idea always to do so. Consistently using var when declaring variables avoids difficulties with variable scope.

We'll be discussing variable scope later in the course, but the short explanation is that there are variables that are only used within a certain segment of your program, such as a function. Variables can be declared so that their value is only retrievable within that scope.

Now that we have declared our variable, we can assign it a value. This is called *variable assignment*.

When we set the initial value of the variable, it is known as *initialization*. Once you have declared your variable, you no longer need to use the var statement. All you need is the name of the variable followed by the equal sign and the value of the variable. In this example, our variable initialization is:

userName="Mark Lassoff";

The value assigned in the above example is a string, also known as text, which is why it was enclosed with quotes. If you are assigning a numerical value to a variable, you do not need to enclose the value with quotes. For example:

age = 39;

A shortcut method for simultaneously declaring and initializing variables is to combine declaration and initialization on the same line. This is a more efficient way of initializing and declaring a variable. Declaring and initializing a variableConcurrently is as follows:

var userName="Mark Lassoff";

We can now display the variable's value. To display the value of the variable you can use the *document.write()* command, followed by the name of the variable in parentheses. The command syntax is:

document.write(userName);

When you want to display the variable's value, you do not need to put quotes around the variable name (like you would if you were outputting text). Instead you simply write the variable name in the parentheses. If it is the actual string value you want to print, then surrounding the string value with quotes is a must. For example:

document.write ("Austin, Texas");

This will display Austin, Texas.

We can also change the value of a variable during the program's execution. Suppose you have displayed the first value assigned to your variable. You then assign another value to the same variable name and then have it displayed. The second value assigned to *userName* replaces the initial value.

So far, we have been assigning values to our variable with the equal sign. However, the equal sign does not mean "equal to" in the context of Javascript. In Javascript, the equal sign is known as the *assignment operator*. The assignment operator merely assigns a value to the variable.

We will discuss more operators and their functions in greater detail later on. The way we read the variable initialization in the previous example is that the variable *userName* was assigned the value Mark

Lassoff. The value being in quotes indicates it as a string value.

When a number is assigned as the value of a variable, it is referred to as a *numeric variable*. This is an example of declaring and assigning a numeric variable:

var userAge= 37;

In the next section, we will use numeric variables to perform some arithmetic operations.

The complete example code listing for the above discussion is presented here, followed by a screenshot of the expected output when viewed in the browser.

Code Listing: Declaring and Assigning Variables

```
<!DOCTYPE HTML PUBLIC "-//W3C//DTD HTML
4.01//EN"

   "http://www.w3.org/TR/html4/strict.dtd" >

<html lang="en">

<head>

</head>

<body>

   <script language="javascript"

       type="text/javascript">
```

```javascript
//var userName="Mark Lassoff";

var     userName;                    //Variable Declaration

    userName="Mark    Lassoff";      //Variables Initialization

        document.write(userName);         //No quotes:  Output value of variables

    userName="Brett Lassoff"; // = Known as the assignment operator

    document.write("<br/>");

    document.write(userName);

    document.write("<br/>");

    var    userAge    =    37;       //Combined initialization/declaration

    document.write(userAge);

  </script>
</body>
</html>
```

This is how the output appears in the browser. Notice how the names and age were displayed on separate lines. This was made possible by using the break *
* tags, along with the *document.write()* command.

Questions for Review

1. In Javascript, what statement do you use to declare a variable?

a. variable

b. declare

c. var

d. dar

2. What happens if you don't put quotes around a variable's string assigned value?

a. The script outputs the value of the variable.

b. You get an HTML error.

c. The script will not assign the variable correctly.

d. Nothing will happen.

3. Which of the following is known as the assignment operator in Javascript?

a. The + sign

b. The = sign

c. The – sign

d. The @ sign

4. Which is an example of combined initialization/declaration?

a. var Size

b. Size = 0

c. var Size; Size = 0;

d. var Size = 0;

5. Why is it important to use the var statement every time you declare a variable?

a. You will have trouble with variable scope if you don't.

b. Variables won't work without being declared.

c. It's confusing without it.

d. You shouldn't use it.

Lab Activity

1) Create a Javascript code that will display the following output:

2) The program must have two variables. The first variable will hold the values for the adult animals, *adultAnimalName*, while the second variable will hold the values for the young animal, *youngAnimalName.*

3) Assign one value to each of the variables. Have these two variable values displayed using *document.write()*.

4) Use the following values for your program:

adultAnimalName	youngAnimalName
Horse	Pony
Goat	Kid
Dog	Puppy

Lab Activity Solution: Code Listing

```
<!DOCTYPE HTML PUBLIC "-//W3C//DTD HTML 4.01//EN"

"http://www.w3.org/TR/html4/strict.dtd"

    >
<html lang="en">
<head>
</head>
<body>
        <script         language="javascript" type="text/javascript">
    var adultAnimalName;
```

```
var youngAnimalName;
adultAnimalName = "Horse";
youngAnimalName = "Pony";
document.write(adultAnimalName);
    document.write(":");
document.write(youngAnimalName);
document.write("<br/>");
adultAnimalName = "Goat";
youngAnimalName = "Kid";
document.write(adultAnimalName);
    document.write(":");
document.write(youngAnimalName);
document.write("<br/>");
adultAnimalName = "Dog";
youngAnimalName = "Puppy";
document.write(adultAnimalName);
    document.write(":");
document.write(youngAnimalName);
document.write("<br/>");
</script>
</body>
```

```
</html>
```

Variable Operators

In this section we are going to discuss variable operators. Once again, start with an HTML 4.01 file, and make sure you include a <script> tag to indicate to the browser that we are using Javascript.

First, we need to declare two variables as *operandOne* and *operandTwo*. These two variables will be assigned the values 125 and 15.371, respectively.

Note that they are two distinct value types. The variable *operandOne* holds the *integer number* 125, while the variable *operandTwo* contains the *floating point number* 15.371. A floating point number is capable of holding numbers with decimal points.

operandOne = 125;

operandTwo = 15.371;

In other programming languages, you would normally have to declare the specific variable type— you have to tell the program if you are using an integer or a floating point number. However, Javascript automatically understands what variable type you are creating the moment you assign its value. There is no need to explicitly specify which type of variable you are using.

With our variables defined and initialized, we can have them displayed as output using the *document.write()* command. Since you are instructing that the program's output be whatever the variable contains, you do not need quotation marks. Let us display the two values on two different lines. The code should be written as follows:

```
document.write (operandOne);

document.write ("<br/>");

document.write (operandTwo);
```

We can also perform arithmetic operations with our variables. To add the two numbers together, we use the addition operator "+". If we want the sum of the two variables displayed, then our code should be:

```
document.write("The sum is " + (operandOne + operandTwo));
```

The addition operator is used twice in this example. The plus (+) sign has two purposes in Javascript—it can be used as a *string concatenation operator,* and also as an *addition operator*. When we write *operandOne + operandTwo*, we are using it to add the two variables.

Concatenation, on the other hand, is also an important operation in any programming language. In Javascript, concatenation joins two strings or values together. In the context of this example, we are concatenating (placing next to each other) the string value "The sum is" to the sum of the two variables. The addition operation is placed within its own parentheses so the program understands that it is a separate operation from the concatenation.

Here is a list of the variable operators you can use and how they function:

Operator	Symbol	**Function**
Addition	+	Adds variables together and concatenates strings and other values.
Subtraction	-	Subtracts the value of one variable from another.
Multiplication	*	Multiplies variables.
Division	/	Divides one variable from another.
Modulus	%	Outputs the remainder of the division operation.

Increment	++	Adds one to the value of the variable.
Decrement	--	Subtracts one from the value of the variable.

The increment and decrement operators function by increasing and decreasing, respectively, the value of the variable by one.

There are two ways to use the increment and decrement operators. When the operator is placed after the variable, it is called a *postfix operator*. This means that the mathematical expression is evaluated and then the increment takes place.

The following code listing provides examples on how each variable operator is used.

Code Listing: Variable Operators

```
<!DOCTYPE HTML PUBLIC "-//W3C//DTD HTML 4.01//EN"

   "http://www.w3.org/TR/html4/strict.dtd"

   >
<html lang="en">

<head>

</head>
```

```html
<body>
        <script          language="javascript"
type="text/javascript">

    var operandOne;

    var operandTwo;

    operandOne = 125;     //Integer

    operandTwo = 15.371;     //Floating Point
Number

    document.write(operandOne);

    document.write("<br/>");

    document.write(operandTwo);

    document.write("<br/>");

    document.write("Addition " + (operandOne +
operandTwo));

    document.write("<br/>");

    document.write("Subtraction " + (operandOne
- operandTwo));

    document.write("<br/>");

        document.write("Multiplication    "    +
(operandOne * operandTwo));

    document.write("<br/>");

        document.write("Division    "    +
(operandOne/operandTwo));
```

```javascript
document.write("<br/>");

document.write("10 % 3 " + (10 % 3));

document.write("<br/>");

document.write("11 % 3 " + (11 % 3));

operandOne++;     //Increment Operator Add One to the variable;

operandTwo--;     //Decrementing One from the variable

document.write("<br/>");

document.write(operandOne);

document.write("<br/>");

document.write(operandTwo);

/*

        variable++     <---   PostFix   Increment Operator

        ++variable     <---   PreFix   Increment Operator

        PostFix- The rest of the mathematical expression is evaluated and then

        the increment takes place

        PreFix-  The increment takes place and then the rest of the expression

        is evaluated
```

```
    */
    var teamCity;

    var teamName;

    teamCity ="New York";

    teamName= "Yankees";

    var fullTeamInfo = teamCity + " " +
teamName;

    document.write("<br/>");

    document.write(fullTeamInfo);

  </script>
</body>
</html>
```

In order to better understand how concatenation works, an example of concatenating two string variables and outputting them is demonstrated within the previous code. We have created a new variable called *fullTeamInfo* and concatenated the two variables *teamCity* and *teamName*. We also concatenated a space within the quotation marks so the two variable strings are spaced properly. The output "New York Yankees" is the result.

This is a screenshot of the output shown in the browser. Here all possible use of concatenation is shown; all four mathematical operations are also demonstrated including the modulus operator.

Questions for Review

1. What does the "+" symbol mean when you place it next to a numerical variable?

a. Add the values together.

b. Take away the values.

c. Concatenate the values.

d. Divide the values.

2. What does the "+" symbol mean when you place it between two string values?

a. Add the values together.

b. Take away the values.

c. Concatenate the values.

d. Divide the values.

3. What does the % operator do?

a. Gives you the sum of division.

b. Gives you the remainder after division.

c. Gives you the multiplication sum.

d. Gives you the subtraction sum.

4. Which is the increment operator?

a. –

b. *

c. ++

d. #

5. How does a prefix increment operator function?

a. It adds one to the variable.

b. The rest of the mathematical expression is evaluated and the increment takes place.

c. It subtracts one from the variable.

d. The increment takes place and then the rest of the expression is evaluated.

1) Create an HTML 4.01 document. In the document body, add script tags with the appropriate attributes to add Javascript code.

2) Declare the following variables (but do not initialize yet):

        firstName
        lastName
        age
        city
        favoriteFood

3) Initialize the variables with information about you. (Your first name, last name, age, etc.)

4) Create a variable called *operand1* and use combined initialization and assignment to assign it an initial value of 1555.

5) Create a variable called *operand2* and use combined initialization and assignment to assign it an initial value of 96.255.

6) Demonstrate your knowledge of the mathematical operators with *operand1* and *operand2* by adding, subtracting, multiplying, and dividing the two values. Format your output as follows:

1555 + 96.255 = 1651.255

The line of code that would produce this output is:

document.write(*operand1* + " + " + *operand2* + " = " + (*operand1*+*operand2*));

7) Demonstrate the use of increment operator with *operand1* and decrement operators with *operand2*. Display the results.

```
<!DOCTYPE HTML PUBLIC "-//W3C//DTD HTML 4.01//EN"

    "http://www.w3.org/TR/html4/strict.dtd"

    >

<html lang="en">

<head>

</head>

<body>

        <script          language="javascript"
type="text/javascript">

    var firstName;

    var lastName;

    var age;

    var city;

    var favoriteFood;

    firstName = "Bob";

    lastName = "Smith";

    age = 45;

    city = "Boston";

    favoriteFood = "Continental";

    var operand1 = 1555;

    var operand2 = 96.255;
```

```
document.write(operand1 +" + "+operand2 +
"=" + (operand1 + operand2));

document.write("<br/>");

document.write(operand1 +" - "+operand2 +
"=" + (operand1 - operand2));

document.write("<br/>");

document.write(operand1 +" x "+operand2 +
"=" + (operand1 * operand2));

document.write("<br/>");

document.write(operand1 +" / "+operand2 +
"=" + (operand1 / operand2));

document.write("<br/>");

document.write("After    increment,    "    +
operand1 + " is now ");

operand1++;

document.write(operand1);

document.write("<br/>");

document.write("After    decrement,    "    +
operand2 + " is now ");

operand2--;

document.write(operand2);

document.write("<br/>");
```

/* Since there were no instructions to display the values of the first five variables that were asked to be declared and assigned, they will not be seen in the output */

    </script>

</body>

</html>

In this chapter we learned about variables, their declaration, initialization, and combined initialization/declaration. You also learned how to output variables.

We also discussed operators, which included the assignment operator and arithmetic operators. You learned that the plus sign (+) can be used as an addition operator or concatenation operator and also learned how to concatenate strings and variables.

Chapter 13. JavaScript Essentials

Since this chapter is quite dense, here's an overview of what you can expect to learn:

- Data types - how JavaScript classifies information. This is important because knowing what type of information you have will also tell you what you can do with that information (e.g., you can't multiply 5 with apples.)

- Comparison Operators - lets you compare certain types of information (e.g., is 5 less than 10?). This is useful when you want to give the computer instructions that relies on certain conditions being met (e.g., allow the user to register only if the age is more than or equal to 18)

- Console.log() - lets you display the output of a single line of code - useful when you want to see how information flows in your program per line of code.

- Flow Control - if-else statements give the computer different instructions to execute depending on which condition is met (e.g., allow the user to enter site if the age is more than 18, otherwise, display an error message)

- Debugging - when your program behaves erratically (e.g., misspelling the user's name or forgetting it completely), then you need to find which part of your code is messing up your program's behavior - this process is called debugging. This can become rather daunting when the code spans more than a thousand lines - knowing where to look will come in handy.

So far, you've played with strings and numbers using JavaScript. In the programming world, these categories of information are referred to as data types.

Data Types

Data types simply tell the computer how your information should be read. For instance, if you type the following into the console:

```
"5" + "5"
```

You'd get "55." This is because by enclosing 5 using quotation marks, you're telling the interpreter that you want 5 to be treated as a string, not a number. The addition operator, then, instead of adding the two numbers, combines the two strings. Now try removing the quotation marks and notice how the output changes to 10. There are different things you can do with different data types, so it's extremely important to know which one to use:

- Strings - Anything you enclose in quotation marks will end up being a string. This can be a combination of letters, spaces, numbers, punctuation marks, and other symbols. Without strings, you wouldn't be able to get the user's name, address, email, and other important details.

- Numbers - Self-explanatory; numbers are the ones you can perform addition, subtraction, multiplication, and division to, among other mathematical operations. Remember not to put quotation marks or you'll turn them into strings!

So far, we now have strings and numbers at our disposal, but remember the console output when you've tried playing with confirmation dialogues? Whenever you press OK, the console returns true, and whenever you press CANCEL, the console returns false. These outputs aren't surrounded by quotation marks, but they surely aren't numbers, so what in the world are they?

- Booleans - booleans are data types that can only be either true or false. This is different from a string or a number, because it helps the computer make decisions based on whether or not certain conditions are met. For example, if you want to prevent minors from registering in your site, you'd have to have some sort of code to separate minors from the adults, like:

```
var age = 17

age >= 18
```

The console, then, returns false because the age is under 18. Now try the following mathematical expressions out and see what you get:

```
5 > 10
```

```
6 < 12
```

The first line should return false, while the second line should return true.

Comparison Operators

So far, we've talked about three data types (numbers, strings, and booleans), as well as some basic mathematical operators (+, -, *, /). What you've just used to test out booleans, however, are comparison operators (<, >, =), which are extremely important in managing the flow of your program. Here's the complete list and what they can do:

> Greater than

< Less than

>= Greater than or equal to

<= Less than or equal to

== Equal to

!= Not equal to

To test out these operators, replace the '@' symbol with the correct operator in the following statements in order to make the console output true:

```
console.log(5 @ 1);

console.log(1 @ 5);

console.log(5 @ 2);

console.log(1 @ 6);

console.log(5 @ 5);

console.log(10 @ 5);
```

Knowing what the Interpreter is Thinking

Notice how the JavaScript interpreter only gives you the latest output of the commands you type in, so if you've typed in three lines of code that should have different outputs:

```
5 > 10
6 < 12
7 > 14
```

Executing them all at the same time in the console, you'd only get the result of the last line (false).

You can, instead, enter each line of code individually so you can see the output of each command, but this gets especially tedious in larger bits of code. When you get to more complicated stuff, you'll eventually run into more errors and bugs. When this happens, you'll want to know what happens in specific commands you give so that you can pinpoint exactly where things go wrong.

console.log() takes whatever code you put inside and logs its execution to the console. That being said, let's see console.log() in action:

```
console.log(5 > 10)
console.log(6 < 12)
```

```
console.log(7 > 14)
```

Now you can see the output of each line of code!

Flow Control

You now know the most basic data types, mathematical operators, comparison operators, and a couple of neat console tricks. In order to make them useful, however, we need to be able to manipulate the flow of commands. For instance, if you wanted to create a user registration form that asks for the user's name, email address, age, and password, you'd first declare the variables as:

```
var name;

var email;

var age;

var password;
```

Now we'd need to store the user's input. For now, we use the prompt function:

```
name = prompt('What's your name?');

email = prompt('What's your email?');
```

```
age = prompt('What's your age?');

password = prompt('Please enter your desired
password: ');
```

Assuming you've entered the right kind of information in the data fields, the name, email, age, and password variables now have the right type of data to process and store. What if, however, the user leaves the email field blank, or the age field with a letter? We can't just let the program continue if some of the vital fields of information don't have the right kind of data, therefore we use flow control statements. The first one we shall discuss is the if statement.

If Statement

If you've already programmed before, the structure of an if statement in JavaScript should be almost identical to the one you're familiar with:

```
if (<condition>)
{
    <action>
}
```

If you haven't already programmed before, an if-statement basically tells the computer to do whatever is inside the curly brackets ({}) if the if condition is true. If we want to, for instance, prevent the user from entering a blank field, we can do the following:

```
name = prompt('What's your name?');

if (name.length == 0)

{

    name = prompt('You cannot leave this empty. What's your name?');

}

email = prompt('What's your email?');

if (email.length == 0)

{

    email = prompt('You cannot leave this empty. What's your email address?');

}

age = prompt('What's your age?');

if (age.length == 0)

{

    age = prompt('You cannot leave this empty. What's your age?');
```

```
}

password = prompt('Please enter your desired
password: ');

if (password.length == 0)

{

    password = prompt('You cannot leave this
empty. Please enter your desired password:');

}
```

The code can seem overwhelming for the first-time programmer, but when you read each line carefully, you'll see that they follow quite a neat and logical structure:

1)   First, since the prompt() function gives you whatever the user types in, you store the string inside a variable so you can use it later in the program.

2)   The if statements check if the variable is empty by checking if the length is equal to zero or not.

A)   IF THE LENGTH IS EQUAL TO ZERO, IT ASKS FOR INPUT AGAIN.

B) IF THE LENGTH ISN'T EQUAL TO ZERO, IT DOESN'T ASK FOR INPUT AGAIN.

Take note that this sample code only serves to illustrate how the if statement works. Under no circumstances should you keep using the prompt() function to ask the user for information.

Now, what if you want to do something else in case your first condition isn't met? For instance, what if you want to say "Your name is <name>. Got it!" after the user types in a valid name? Then we add an else condition, followed by a second pair of curly braces that enclose the second set of commands:

```
name = prompt('What's your name?');

if (name.length == 0)

{

    name = prompt('You cannot leave this empty. What's your name?');

}

else
```

```javascript
{
    alert('Your name is ' + name + '. Got it!');
}
email = prompt('What's your email?');
if (email.length == 0)
{
    email = prompt('You cannot leave this empty.
What's your email address?');
}
else
{
    alert('Your email is ' + email + '. Got it!');
}
age = prompt('What's your age?');
if (age.length == 0)
{
    age = prompt('You cannot leave this empty.
What's your age?');
}
else
{
```

```
    alert('Your age is ' + age + '. Got it!');

}

password = prompt('Please enter your desired
password: ');

if (password.length == 0)

{

    password = prompt('You cannot leave this
empty. Please enter your desired password:');

}

else

{

    alert('Your password is ' + password + '. Got
it!');

}
```

Now your code sounds a little more human, as it responds better to user input. Try messing around with the code and see how the interpreter changes the output depending on the conditions met with the if-else statements.

Debugging

So far, you've managed to play around with variables, data types, mathematical operators, comparison operators, user prompts, confirmation dialogues, and alerts, and lastly, if-else statements. Don't worry if you make a couple of mistakes; computers are intrinsically literal and will not tolerate the tiniest syntactical mistakes. That being said, here are a couple of codes that don't seem to work as intended. Change the following code snippets so that you can produce the appropriate output!

```
var name = "Chris";

alert('Hi ' + 'name' + '! It's nice to meet you.');
```

In this code snippet, the output is supposed to be "Hi Chris! It's nice to meet you." What's the current output and what do you think is wrong with the code? Notice that the console doesn't complain and throw you an error message when you execute this code. This kind of problem is called a 'bug,' because while the JavaScript interpreter sees nothing wrong with this code, it doesn't work as the creator intended.

Now try to correct this code snippet that contains both bugs and errors:

```
var name;

var age;

name = prompt('What's your name?');
```

```
if (name.length = 0);

{

    name = prompt('You cannot leave this empty.
What's your name?');

}

else (name.length != 0)

{

    alert('Your name is ' + name + '. Got it!');

}

age = prompt('What's your age?');

if (age.length = 0)

{

    age = prompt('You cannot leave this empty.
What's your age?');

}

else (name.length != 0)

{

    alert('Your age is ' + age + '. Got it!');

}
```

This code is a distorted version of a previous sample code, so you may try to compare the codes and see why this one doesn't work. If you feel stuck, you can check out a program called 'linter,' which is a handy tool that checks your code for errors and tells you which lines have them. It's good exercise to practice your debugging skills now, because when you create more complex programs, debugging becomes almost routine.

What to look for when debugging:

Looking for bugs and errors can be quite overwhelming if you don't know where to look. Here are some of the most common mistakes programmers make when coding:

- Using '=' instead of '==' to compare two values - the '=' sign in programming is used as an assignment operator, which means that if you use this instead of the '==' sign, you end up replacing the value of the variable on the left hand side of the equation with the value on the right hand side of the equation.

- Misplacing the semicolon - just as periods end sentences in the English language, semicolons end statements in JavaScript, as well as other programming languages like C, Java, etc. If, for instance, you've accidentally put a semicolon in the middle of a statement,

JavaScript would see the statement as incomplete and produce an error for it.

- Misusing the quotation marks - quotation marks tell the interpreter that you're using a string, so if you enclose a variable or a number in quotation marks, you're effectively turning them into strings. This'll lead to anomalies when you try to perform numerical operations onto numbers that you've accidentally enclosed in quotation marks.

So far, these are only the most common mistakes newbies tend to make, but along the way you should be able to see bugs and errors quite easily as you get more practice making more complex codes.

Recap

We've covered quite a lot of concepts so far, so let's review what we've learned:

- Variables and data types

○   *numbers - can be integers or numbers that contain decimals (e.g., 3.14, 5, 100)*

○   *strings - anything you enclose in quotation marks (e.g., "5", "I am a JavaScript master", "I love the number 7")*

○   *booleans - true or false*

In order to declare a variable, simply type:

```
var <variable name> = <value>;
```

You can also just declare the variable name without the value if you don't have one yet:

```
var <variable name>;
```

JavaScript doesn't care what type of data you put in. If you've programmed in C or Java, you might have been used to declaring the variable's data type (int, float, char, etc.), but in JavaScript, you can put anything in a variable without any problems.

Chapter 4 Pop-up boxes

○ *alert("Hi There!") - you can pop-up alerts to the user.*

○ *confirm("Are you sure?") - you can ask for a confirmation from the user.*

○ *prompt("Type anything here.") - you can ask for input from the user*

- Flow-control

○ *if-else statement - in a nutshell, if the first condition is met, then do whatever's in the first bracket enclosure and skip the 'else' part.*

*Otherwise, go to the bracket enclosure for the 'else'
condition and do whatever's inside it.*

Chapter 14. Regular Expressions

What are regular expressions?

Regular expressions represent a pattern. In JavaScript, regular expressions can be used to perform operations such as searching a pattern, replacing a pattern, checking if a string matches a given pattern or breaking of a string into smaller strings based on a specific pattern. In JavaScript, regular expressions are objects.

Making a regular expression

There are two ways by which you can create regular expressions in JavaScript, which are:

8. Using regular expression literal:

In this method, the pattern is specified within two slashes // followed by the character(s) which are known as modifiers. You will learn about what modifiers are later in this chapter; modifiers are optional.
Syntax:

/pattern/modifiers

/pattern/

If this method is used, then the regular expression is compiled when the script is loaded and thus if the regular expression is constant, this method improves the performance of the program.

- **Using constructor of RegExp object:**

    In this method, we use the 'new' keyword to initialize a new object of RegExp which stands for Regular Expression. The pattern is passed as the first argument to the RegExp constructor and the modifier as the second argument, note that the modifier argument here is optional too.

    Syntax:

new RegExp("pattern", "modifiers");

new RegExp("pattern");

If this method is used, then the regular expression is compiled at runtime, this method is generally used where regular expression is not a constant.

MODIFIERS

A modifier is used to change the way a match of pattern based on regular expression is done. Listed below are the modifiers and the details on how they affect the operation.

- i

    Makes the match case insensitive, by default matching done is with regular expressions is case sensitive.

- m

Makes the match of pattern extend to multiple lines one if there are more than one lines in the string that the match is being performed on.

2. g

By default, the operation stops after finding the first match for the pattern, but if this modifier is used the operations don't stop at the first match and thus performs a 'g'lobal match.

Simple patterns

If you want to match a sequence of character directly, then you can write it in the place of the pattern. For example, the regular expression /test/ will match any string with 'test' in it, so there would be a match for a string like 'this is a test, ' but there would not be any match for string like 'this is a est' because the character 't' is missing from the sequence specified.

Certain characters denotes something special in a regular expression like '*' or '.', if you want to match these characters directly then you need to escape them, i.e., add a backslash before them. So for matching the exact string 'te*st', the regular expression will be /te*st/. You will learn about all the characters with a special significance in regular expressions in the very next section.

Special character(s)

Here is a list of special character(s) that can be used for a regular expression and what they do:

- ^

  If present at the start of the regular expression, this character signifies that the following pattern should be matched from the beginning of the input. If the 'm' modifier is used, then the starting of each line is also tested for the match.

  For example, the regular expression /^test/ will not match anything in the string 'this is a test' as 'test' is not present at the beginning of the string, but the same regular expression will match with the string 'test is going on'.

- $

  If present at the end of the regular expression, this character signifies that the pattern should be matched with the end of the line. If the 'm' modifier is used then the end of each line is tested for the match.

  For example, the regular expression /test$/ will not match anything in the string 'test is going on' as 'test' is not present at the end of the string, but the same regular expression will match the string 'this is a test.'

- *

  This character is used to match the expression preceding this character zero or more times.

  For example, the regular expression /te*st/ will match 't' followed by zero or more 'e' and that followed by 'st', so the string 'this is a teeeeeest' as well as the string 'this is a tst' will be matched but the string 'this is teees' won't be matched since a 't' is missing from the sequence to be matched.

Chapter 2 +

  This character is used to match the expression preceding this character one or more times, i.e., if the preceding expression occurs at-least once.

  For example, the regular expression /te*st/ will match the string 'this is a teeeeeest' but won't match the string 'this is a tst' or the string 'this is a tees'.

- ?

  This character is used to match the expression preceding this character zero or one time.

  For example, the regular expression /te?st/ will match the string 'this is a test' and 'this is a tst' but won't match the string 'this is a teest' or the string 'this is a tes'.

- {x}

This form of expression is used to match exactly x occurrences of the preceding expression, where x is a positive integer.

For example, the regular expression /te{3}st/ will match the string 'this is a teeest' but won't match the string 'this is a test' or the string 'this is a teeeeest'.

3. {x, y}

This form of expression is used to match any number of occurrences between x and y of the preceding expression, where x and y both are positive integers and x is less than or equal to y.

For example, the regular expression /te{3, 6}st/ will match the string 'this is a teeest' and 'this is a teeeeest' but won't match the string 'this is a test' or the string 'this is a teeeeeeest'.

- {x, }

This form of expression is used to match at-least x occurrences of the preceding expression, where x is a positive integer.

For example, the regular expression /te{3,}st/ will match the string 'this is a teeest' but won't match the string 'this is a test' or the string 'this is a teest'.

- .

This character is used to match any character except a newline one.

For example, the regular expression /te.st/ will match the string 'this is a tOst' and 'this is a tZst' but won't match the string 'this is a tst'.

- [abc]

This form of expression is used to match any character or expression that is present between the square brackets.

For example, the regular expression /t[eyz]st/ will match the string 'this is a test' and 'this is a tzst' but won't match the string 'this is a tpst' or the string 'this is a trst'.

You can use ranges like a-z and 0-9 which matches all the character from 'a' to 'z' and '0' to '9' respectively.For example, the regular expression /t[a-z]st/ will match the string 'this is a test' and 'this is a tkst' but won't match the string 'this is a t9st' or the string 'this is a t2st', but the regular expression /t[a-z0-9]st/ will match all the strings mentioned in this particular example.

- [^abc]

This form of expression is used to match anything EXCEPT the character(s) or expression(s) that is present between the [^ and].

For example, the regular expression /t[^eyz]st/ will match the string 'this is a tpst' and 'this is a trst' but won't match the string 'this is a test' or the string 'this is a tyst'.

You can use the ranges, just like in the above-mentioned expression, in this form of expression too.For example, the regular expression /t[^a-z]st/ will match the string 'this is a t9st' and 'this is a t8st' but won't match the string 'this is a test' or the string 'this is a tast'.

- (abc)

This form of expression is called a capture group. The pattern between the () is matched normally but is stored in memory for later use; you will learn about this expression usage in methods like .exec() later in this chapter.

Meta Characters

These are the special character sequences that are used to match certain characters or range of characters. Some of the most used metacharacters are:

- \w

    Matches any word character, i.e., any alphanumeric character including underscore.

    - \W

    Matches any non-word character. All the characters that are not matched by \w are matched by this.

    - \d

Matches any digit, i.e., any character from 0 to 9.

- **\D**

  Matches any non-digit, i.e., any character except from 0 to 9.

- **\w**

  Matches any whitespace character, i.e., characters like tab, space, line ends etc.

- **\W**

  Matches any non-whitespace character, i.e., any character except whitespace characters like tab, space, line ends, etc.

Using regular expressions

Now that you have learned about how to make up a regular expression, we can move on to learn about how to put them into action. Listed below are the methods which you can use with a regular expression.

- regexObject.test(string)

  This method tries to match the regular expression with the string passed as the argument, if it is matched, this method returns true else false.

  Examples:

var result1 = /example/.test('this is an example');

var result2 = /example/.test('what is this');

console.log(result1); //prints 'true' on the console screen

cosnole.log(result2);//prints 'false' on the console screen

- regexObject.exec(string)
  This method tries to match the regular expression with the string passed as the argument, if it is matched, this method returns an array filled with information else it returns null. The returned array first item is the matched string and the second is the first capture group present if any and third item is the second capture group present if any and so on.
  Examples:

var result1 = /exam(pl)e/.test('this is an example');

var result2 = /example/.test('what is this');

console.log(result1[0]); //prints 'example' on the console screen

console.log(result[1]); //prints 'pl' on the console screen

cosnole.log(result2); //prints 'null' on the console screen

2. string.search(regex)

This method tries to find a match of the regex passed as the argument. If found, it returns the index(position) of the match else returns -1. Note that the index begins from 0, not from 1. So the first character's index in a string is 0 and the second character's index is 1.

Examples:

```
var result1 = 'an example'.search(/a.p/);

var result2 = 'an example'.search(/55/);

console.log( result ); //prints '5' on the console screen

cosnole.log( result2 ); //prints '-1' on the console screen
```

2. `string.replace(regex, replacer)`

This method tries to find a match of regex passed as the first argument if found it replaces the match with the second argument(replacer).

Example:

```
var original = "this is an example";

//replcaes first s and a with 9

var new = original.replace(/[sa]/, '9');
```

//replcaes each s and a with 9, since the'g' modifier is used

var new2 = original.replace(/[sa]/g, '9');

console.log(new);//prints 'thi9 is an example' on the console screen

console.log(new2);//prints 'thi9 i9 9n ex9mple' on the console screen

> We can also use capture groups in the regular expression in this function and then use them in the replacer string. If in the replacer string we use a $ sign followed by a number then that $ sign with the number is replaced by the capture group of that index. For example, $1 gets replaced by the first capture group in the regular expression and $2 by the second one and so on. Example:

var original = "this is an example";

//places _ on both side of each s and a

var new = original.replace(/([sa])/g, '_$1_');

console.log(new);//prints   'thi_s_   i_s_   _a_n ex_a_mple' on the console screen

In this chapter, you have learned about regular expressions. I hope you have got a basic idea of regular expressions in JavaScript after reading this chapter.

Hoisting

What is hoisting?

The word hoist means to lift or raise up by means of some mechanical device like a pulley, but in JavaScript, hoisting means that the functions and variable declarations are moved to the top of the scope or context they are declared in, i.e., lifted up as in hoist, thus the word 'hoist'ing.

The declarations aren't really moved to the top, they are just put first into the compiled code.

Variable hoisting

For example the following code:

```
x = 21;

console.log( x );

var x;
```

Really compiles as this:

```
var x;

x = 21;

  console.log(x);
```

As you can see the declaration has moved to the top of the current context, this is what hoisting is.

Let's understand this with a more suitable example:

```
console.log( x ); // prints 'undefined' on the
console screen

console.log( y ); // throws a ReferenceError
saying 'y is not defined'

var x;
```

This happens because 'x' being declared in the current context, though it is below the console.log line, it is moved at the top of the context and as there is no assignment done to 'x', it is set to 'undefined' by default, whereas in case of 'y' it is not available anywhere in current context, therefore, a ReferenceError is thrown.

Note that the assignment operation is not hoisted, only the declaration is.

Example:

```
console.log(x); //prints 'undefined' on the
console screen

var x; // only this statement is hoisted

x = 21; // this is not
```

You must be wondering about, what if we assign the value to variable while declaring it, like 'var x = 21;', though here it seems that you are assigning value to variable while declaring it but in fact internally the variable is first declared and then the value is assigned to it, so it is equivalent to 'var x; x = 21;'. So if you declare a variable like this below the line where it is being used but in the same context then only declaration part is hoisted.

Example:

> console.log(x);   //prints 'undefined' on the console screen
>
> var x = 21;

This is how the above code is compiled:

> var x;
>
> console.log(x);   //prints 'undefined' on the console screen

x = 21;

Function hoisting

Just as variable hoisting, functions are also hoisted. As a result the functions can be called even before they are declared, given that it is declared in the current context or scope.

Example:

> test();
>
> function test() {
>
> console.log('This is a test');
>
}

> //prints 'This is a test' on the console screen

It is to be noted that function expressions, i.e., functions that are assigned to variables through the assignment operator '=' are not hoisted. The case of

413

hoisting function expression is same as assigning a value a variable, which has been discussed above.

Example:

Just as variable

test(); // throws a TypeError saying 'test is not a function'

testRandom(); // throws ReferenceError saying 'testRandom is not defined'

var test = function {

console.log('This is a test');

};

In the above example, the difference in types of error is caused due to hoisting. As visible the variable 'test' is declared in the current scope therefore its declaration is moved at top and hence it is declared, though its value is undefined at the point where it is used, so a TypeError is thrown which indicates that the 'test' is defined but is not a function, whereas the function 'testRandom' is not declared anywhere, so a ReferenceError is thrown.

Order of precedence of hoisting

Functions are always hoisted over variable declaration.

Example:

function test() {

```
    //function code

  }
var test;

    console.log( typeof test ); //prints 'function' on
    the console screen
```

Even if the position of the variable line and function line are swapped in the above example, the output will remain the same.

But functions are not hoisted over variable declaration, given the assignment is done above the line where it is being used.

Example:

```
    function test() {

    //function code

  }
    var test = 21; //now assignment is being done
    too
    console.log( typeof test ); //prints 'number' on
    the console screen
```

Even if the position of the variable line and function line are swapped in the above example, the output will remain the same.

As mentioned this is valid as long as the assignment is done above the line where it is being used, when the assignment is done below, then the function is hoisted over the assignment.

Example:

```
function test() {
//function code
}
var test;
console.log(typeof test);//prints 'function' on the console screen
test = 21;
console.log(typeof test);//prints 'number' on the console screen
```

CONCLUSION

It is always the best practice to declare variables or functions on the top of the scope where they will be used to avoid any confusion, even though due to hoisting variable declaration will be moved to the top of the scope or context automatically.

Chapter 15. Basic Data Types of Variables

Variables have four basic data types. These are numbers, strings, Boolean, and objects. We'll skim through these types, because going in-depth in discussing them will leave us not time in learning your JavaScript basic codes.

- Numbers

In JavaScript, generally, all numbers are considered as 64-bit floating point numbers. When there are no values after the decimal point, the number is presented as a whole number.

Examples:

- 9.000 is presented as 9

- 6.000 is presented as 6

- 2.00 is presented as 2

JavaScript and other computer programming languages are based on the IEEE 754 standard, or the Standard for Floating-Point Arithmetic.

Number literals can be a floating-point number, an integer or a hexadecimal.

Example of floating-point numbers:

- 4.516

- 9.134

- 6.01

- 4.121

Examples of integers:
- 34

- 45

- 21

- 30

Examples of hexadecimal numbers
- **OxFF**

- **-OxCCFF**

Special number values
- 'NAN' AND 'INFINITY' - are JavaScript's two 'error values'

The NaN (Not a Number) error appears when the browser cannot parse the number, or when an operation failed.

On the other hand, Infinity is an error that appears when the number cannot be represented because of its magnitude. The error also appears when you divide a number by zero (0).

- -0 AND +0 – the -0 rarely appears, so don't get confused about these special number values. You can ignore them, for now.

- NULL – these are obtained when the browser cannot return a value.

2. Strings

Strings are data types that are typically enclosed in matching single quotes or double quotes. The elements can be numbers or texts.

- Boolean

These data types represent either 'true' or 'false'. Through the use of Boolean, you can find out whether a JavaScript expression is 'true' or 'false'.

The 'true' returns are generally obtained from expressions with true values, such as number equations and similar expressions.

In contrast, 'false' returns are obtained from expressions without true values.

EXAMPLE 1:

(3 > 9)

Of course, this is false because 9 is definitely greater than 3.

Example 2:

(2<3)
Obviously, the statement is 'true'. There's no need for an explanation on that one.

EXAMPLE 3:

(4=9)

A 'ReferenceError' will occurre on the third example. This is because in JavaScript language, and most computer programming language, the equal sign (=) is not a symbol of equality. The equal sign is used in assigning the values or elements of variables.

See next image:

When the correct JavaScript syntax was utilized, the expression returned with a 'false' value because even with the correct sign, 4 is still not equal to 9.

- Objects

Objects encompass all data types in the sense that numbers, Booleans, and strings can be objects. Data, such as arrays, regular expressions, dates and math are objects, as well

Objects contain many values and have properties (name:values pair) and methods (process or action). Thus, they are containers of named values. This name:values pair is called property (name) and property values (values).

They can be a collection of various different data.

EXAMPLES:

- student: "Johnson"

- country: "Sweden"

- street: "Reed Avenue"

EXAMPLE:

var students =
{firstName: "Lena", lastName: "Dean"};

SEE IMAGE BELOW:

They are typically expressed in pairs as 'name:value'. Take note of the colon in between the pair, and the commas after each pair. The property values are in quotes, and the entire statement is in brackets.

Chapter 16. The window object

What is the 'window' object?
As the name suggests, this object represents the current window. All major parts of the BOM are the direct children of this object. For example, window.document (The DOM), window.history, etc. Note that each tab on the browser has a unique window object. They don't share the same object! Some properties like window size, which is the same in all tabs, have the same value and technically those properties are shared. The window object contains references to useful properties and functions that may not strictly be related to the window only.

Even though there is no strict standard for the 'window' object, it is supported by all browsers.

The default references to the 'window' object
Since the 'window' object is present on top of hierarchy with no other object present at its level, all references to the window object's methods and properties can be made without writing the starting of the dotted notation part, i.e., the 'window.' part. Example:

WINDOW.ALERT()

alert()// same as above

var x = window.length;

var y = length;

// x will be equal to y since the refer to the same property
All variables declared are actually 'window' object's properties
As stated above, even the variables declared in the program are the direct child of the 'window' object, and are its properties.

Example:

var x = 21;

console.log(window.x); // prints '21' on the console screen

The 'window' object's method references
Here is the list of the 'window' object's major methods and their description:

- .ALERT("MESSAGE")

This method is used to display a dialog box on the screen, a type of pop-up, with a message that is passed as the argument of this function. The dialog box this will open has only one button, which is "OK"

Example:

window.alert(" Hello from JavaScript! ")

OR

alert(" Hello from JavaScript! ")

Both of the above statements are equivalent.

- .CONFIRM("MESSAGE")

This method is used to display a dialog box on the screen, with a message that is passed as the argument of this function, along with two buttons which are "OK" and "Cancel". This method returns a boolean value. It returns true if the "OK" button was clicked and false if the "Cancel" button was clicked.

Example:

var val = confirm(" Do you accept our terms and agreement? ");

if(val == true) console.log("User pressed OK");

else console.log("User pressed Cancel");

- **.prompt("message", "default text")**

This method is used to display a dialog box on the screen, with a message and an input box where the user can enter a value, along with the "OK" and "Cancel" button. This method is used to take an input from the user. The 'default text' parameter is the default value of the input box in the dialog box. This method returns the value entered by the user in the input box if the user presses the "OK" button. If the user presses the "Cancel" button, this method returns 'null'.

Example:

var val = prompt("What is your name?", "Enter your name here");

if(val === null) console.log("User pressed the cancel button");

else console.log("User's name is " + val);

- **.open([URL,] [name,] [specs,] [replace])**

This method is used to open a new window. All the parameters in this method are optional. This method returns the window object of the newly created window. Here is the description of the parameters:

→ URL

This parameter is used to specify the URL of the page to be opened in the new window. The default value of this parameter is 'about:blank' which opens a window with a blank page.

→ NAME

This parameter is used to specify how the URL is opened in the window or the name of the window. The following values are used as this parameter:

❖ **'_blank'**: This is the default value of the 'name' parameter. If this value is used, the URL is loaded in a new window.

❖ **'_parent'**: If this value is used, the URL is loaded in the parent frame.

❖ **'_top'**: If this value is used, the URL replaces any of the framesets that have been loaded previously.

❖ **'_self'**: If this value is used, the URL replaces the current page and is loaded in the current page.

❖ **Any other value**: If any other value is used, it acts as the name of the window. Note that the name of the window is not the same as the title of the window.

➜ SPECS

This parameter is a string which contains some attributes, separated by a comma, of the new window to be opened. You can specify things such as width, height etc. of the new window using this parameter.

➜ REPLACE

This parameter specifies whether the new URL to be opened will replace the current URL in the history object list or not. It takes boolean values, true or false. If 'true' is passed as the value of this parameter, the new URL replaces the current URL in the history object list. If 'false' is passed, it does not.

Example:

var newWindow = window.open("http://mySite.com", "", "height=210,width=700"); // creates a new window with 210px height and 700px width.

- .CLOSE()

This method is used to close a window.

Example:

var newWindow =
window.open("http://mySite.com");
newWindow.close(); // closes the window as soon as it opens

- **.scrollTo(xCoords, yCoords)**

This method is used to set the scroll of the window to the specified coordinates in the document.

- **.resizeTo(height, width)**

This method is used to resize the window to a specified height and width. The height and width passed as the parameters in this argument are in pixels(px).

The 'window' object's properties
Here is the list of the 'window' object's major properties and their description:

- .PAGEXOFFSET

This property returns the current horizontal scroll distance in pixels(px). It is basically the **horizontal** distance between the actual left corner of the page and the current window left corner.

- .SCROLLX

Same as the window.pageXOffset property.

- .PAGEYOFFSET

This property returns the current vertical scroll distance in pixels(px). It is basically the **vertical** distance between the actual left corner of the page and the current window left corner.

- .SCROLLY

Same as the window.pageYOffset property.

- .OUTERHEIGHT

This property returns the full height of the window, including the document, the toolbar, and the scrollbar.

- .OUTERWIDTH

This property returns the full width of the window, including the document, the toolbar, and the scrollbar.

- .INNERHEIGHT

This property returns the height of the content area of the window where the HTML document is displayed. It does **not** include the scrollbar or toolbar height.

- .INNERWIDTH

This property returns the width of the content area of the window where the HTML document is displayed. It does **not** include the scrollbar or toolbar height.

- .FRAMES

Returns an array of all the <iframe> element's in the current window if any.

Example:

<body>

    <iframe
src="https://mySite1.com"></iframe>

    <iframe
src="https://mySite2.com"></iframe>

<SCRIPT>

console.log(window.frames.length); // prints '2' on the console screen
</SCRIPT>

</body>

- .CLOSED

Returns a boolean value indicating whether a window has been closed or not. If the returned value is true, the window has been closed. If false, the window has not been closed.

Example:

var newWindow =
window.open("http://mySite.com");

function isNewWindowOpen()

{

if(newWindow.closed == true)return "NO";

else return "YES";

}

Chapter 17. Maps and Sets

The map class is used to hold a set of key value pairs. The values can be primitive types (like numbers or strings) or object types. The syntax for declaring the map object is shown below.

```
var mapname=new Map();
```

Where 'mapname' is the name of the new map object. To add a key value pair to the Map, you can use the 'set' method as shown below.

mapname.set(key,value)

Where 'key' is the key for the key value pair and 'value' is the subsequent value for the key. To get a value from the map, we can use the 'get' method to get the value for the subsequent key.

Let's look at a way maps can be used through an example.

Example 64: The following program is used to showcase how to use a map class in JavaScript.

The following things need to be noted about the above program:

- We first declare a map object by using the 'new' clause and using the 'map' class.

- Next we set a key/value pair by using the 'set' method.

- Finally we display the value for the key by using the 'get' method.

With this program, the output is as follows:

JavaScript Program

The value for key1 is value1

Let's look at another example of using maps, this time using multiple keys and values.

Example 65: The following program shows how to use a map class with multiple key value pairs.

```
<!DOCTYPE html>
<html>
<body>
  <h2>JavaScript Program</h2>

    <p id="demo1"></p>

    <p id="demo2"></p>

    <p id="demo3"></p>
<script>
```

```
var map=new Map();

map.set("key1","value1");

map.set("key2","value2");

map.set("key3","value3");

document.getElementById("demo1").innerHTML
= "The value for key1 is "+map.get("key1");

document.getElementById("demo2").innerHTML
= "The value for key2 is "+map.get("key2");

document.getElementById("demo3").innerHTML
= "The value for key3 is "+map.get("key3");

</script>

</body>

</html>
```

With this program, the output is as follows:
JavaScript Program

The value for key1 is value1

The value for key2 is value2

The value for key3 is value3

There are multiple methods available for the map class. Let's look at them in more detail.

Table 3: Map Properties and Methods

Property	Description
size	This is used to display the number of elements in the map
clear	This is used to clear all the elements in the map
delete	This is used to delete an element in the map
has	This is used to check if a map has a particular element or not
keys	This is used to get the keys of the map collection
values	This is used to get the values of the map collection

size Property

The 'size' property is used to display the number of elements in the map. Let's now look at an example of this property.

Example 66: The following program is used to showcase how to use the size property.

```
<!DOCTYPE html>

<html>

<body>

  <h2>JavaScript Program</h2>

    <p id="demo1"></p>

<script>

var map=new Map();

map.set("key1","value1");

map.set("key2","value2");

map.set("key3","value3");

document.getElementById("demo1").innerHTML
= "The number of elements in the map
"+map.size;

</script>

</body>

</html>
```

With this program, the output is as follows:

JavaScript Program

The number of elements in the map 3

clear Method

The 'clear' method is used to clear all the elements in the map. Let's now look at an example of this method.

Example 67: The following program is used to showcase how to use the clear method.

```
<!DOCTYPE html>
<html>
<body>

  <h2>JavaScript Program</h2>

    <p id="demo1"></p>

    <p id="demo2"></p>
<script>
var map=new Map();
map.set("key1","value1");
map.set("key2","value2");
map.set("key3","value3");
document.getElementById("demo1").innerHTML
= "The number of elements in the map
"+map.size;
map.clear();
```

```
document.getElementById("demo2").innerHTML
= "The number of elements in the map
"+map.size;
```

</script>

</body>

</html>

With this program, the output is as follows:

JavaScript Program

The number of elements in the map 3

The number of elements in the map 0

delete Method

The 'delete' method is used to delete an element in the map. Let's now look at an example of this method.

Example 68: The following program is used to showcase how to use the delete method.

```
<!DOCTYPE html>
```

<html>

<body>

```
  <h2>JavaScript Program</h2>

    <p id="demo1"></p>

    <p id="demo2"></p>
```

```
<script>

var map=new Map();

map.set("key1","value1");

map.set("key2","value2");

map.set("key3","value3");

document.getElementById("demo1").innerHTML
= "The number of elements in the map
"+map.size;

map.delete("key2");

document.getElementById("demo2").innerHTML
= "The number of elements in the map
"+map.size;

</script>

</body>

</html>
```

With this program, the output is as follows:

JavaScript Program

The number of elements in the map 3

The number of elements in the map 2

has Method

The 'has' method is used to check if a map has a particular element or not. Let's now look at an example of this method.

Example 69: The following program is used to showcase how to use the has method.

```
<!DOCTYPE html>
<html>
<body>

  <h2>JavaScript Program</h2>

    <p id="demo1"></p>

    <p id="demo2"></p>
<script>
var map=new Map();
map.set("key1","value1");
map.set("key2","value2");
map.set("key3","value3");
document.getElementById("demo1").innerHTML
= "The number of elements in the map
"+map.size;

document.getElementById("demo2").innerHTML
= "Does the map have the element key2 "
+map.has("key2");
</script>
</body>
</html>
```

With this program, the output is as follows:

JavaScript Program

The number of elements in the map 3

Does the map have the element key2 true

keys Method

The 'keys' method is used to acquire the keys of the map collection. Let's now look at an example of this method.

Example 70: The following program is used to showcase how to use the keys method.

```
<!DOCTYPE html>
<html>
<body>

  <h2>JavaScript Program</h2>

    <p id="demo1"></p>
<script>
var map=new Map();
map.set("key1","value1");
map.set("key2","value2");
map.set("key3","value3");
var text="";
for (var key of map.keys())
```

```
{

  text+=key;

  text+="</br>";

 }

document.getElementById("demo1").innerHTML
= text;
```
</script>

</body>

</html>

With this program, the output is as follows:

JavaScript Program

key1

key2

key3

values Method

The 'values' method is used to get the values of the map collection. Let's now look at an example of this method.

Example 71: The following program is used to showcase how to use the values method.

```
<!DOCTYPE html>
<html>
<body>

  <h2>JavaScript Program</h2>

    <p id="demo1"></p>
<script>
var map=new Map();
map.set("key1","value1");
map.set("key2","value2");
map.set("key3","value3");
var text="";
for (var value of map.values())

  {

    text+= value;

    text+="</br>";

  }
document.getElementById("demo1").innerHTML
= text;
</script>
</body>
</html>
```

With this program, the output is as follows:

<u>JavaScript Program</u>

value1

value2

value3

<u>set Class</u>

The 'set' class lets you store unique values of any type. The values can be primitive types, such as numbers and strings, or object types. The syntax for declaring the 'set' object is shown below.

```
var setname=new Set();
```

Where 'setname' is the name of the new set object. To add a value to the set, you can use the 'add' method as shown below.

setname.add(value)

To check whether the set has a value we can use the 'has' method. Let's look at a way sets can be used through an example.

Example 72: The following program is used to showcase how to use a set class in JavaScript.

```
<!DOCTYPE html>

<html>
```

443

```
<body>

  <h2>JavaScript Program</h2>

    <p id="demo1"></p>

<script>

var set=new Set();

set.add("value1");

set.add("value2");

set.add("value3");

var text="";

document.getElementById("demo1").innerHTML
= "Does the set contain value2
"+set.has("value2");

</script>

</body>

</html>
```

With this program, the output is as follows:

JavaScript Program

Does the set contain value2 true

Table 4: Set Properties and Methods

Property	Description
size	This is used to display the number of elements in the set
clear	This is used to clear all the elements in the map
delete	This is used to delete an element in the map
values	This is used to get the values of the map collection

size Property

The 'size' property is used to display the number of elements in the set. Let's look at an example of this property.

Example 73: The following program is used to showcase how to use the size property.

```
<!DOCTYPE html>
<html>
<body>

 <h2>JavaScript Program</h2>
```

```
    <p id="demo1"></p>
<script>

var set=new Set();

set.add("value1");

set.add("value2");

set.add("value3");

var text="";

document.getElementById("demo1").innerHTML
= "The number of elements is "+ set.size;

</script>

</body>

</html>
```

With this program, the output is as follows:
JavaScript Program

The number of elements is 3

clear Method

The 'clear' method is used to clear all the elements in the set. Let's now look at an example of this method.

Example 74: The following program is used to showcase how to use the clear method.

446

```
<!DOCTYPE html>
<html>
<body>

 <h2>JavaScript Program</h2>

   <p id="demo1"></p>

   <p id="demo2"></p>
<script>
var set=new Set();
set.add("value1");
set.add("value2");
set.add("value3");
document.getElementById("demo1").innerHTML
= "The number of elements is "+ set.size;
set.clear();
document.getElementById("demo2").innerHTML
= "The number of elements is "+ set.size;
</script>
</body>
</html>
```

With this program, the output is as follows:

JavaScript Program

The number of elements is 3

The number of elements is 0

9.10 delete Method

The 'delete' method is used to delete an element in the set. Let's now look at an example of this method.

Example 75: The following program is used to showcase how to use the delete method.

```
<!DOCTYPE html>
<html>
<body>

  <h2>JavaScript Program</h2>

    <p id="demo1"></p>

    <p id="demo2"></p>

<script>

var set=new Set();

set.add("value1");

set.add("value2");

set.add("value3");
```

```
document.getElementById("demo1").innerHTML
= "The number of elements is "+ set.size;

set.delete("value2");

document.getElementById("demo2").innerHTML
= "The number of elements is "+ set.size;

</script>

</body>

</html>
```

With this program, the output is as follows:

JavaScript Program

The number of elements is 3

The number of elements is 2

9.11 values Method

The 'values' method is used to get the values of the set collection. Let's quickly look at an example of this method.

Example 76: The following program is used to showcase how to use the values method.

```
<!DOCTYPE html>

<html>

<body>

 <h2>JavaScript Program</h2>
```

```
<p id="demo1"></p>
<script>
var set=new Set();
set.add("value1");
set.add("value2");
set.add("value3");
var text="";
for (var value of set.values())
  {
    text+=value;
    text+="</br>";
  }
document.getElementById("demo1").innerHTML
= text;
</script>
</body>
</html>
```

With this program, the output is as follows:
JavaScript Program

value1
value2
value3

450

Conclusion

In this book, I have provided you with the basic knowledge that you will need to start your journey in programming using JavaScript. The different concepts taught here, such as functions, loops, branches, and objects will equip you with the skills that you need to create your first JavaScript project.

Also, continue practicing and taking on small projects to start improving your skills. Through the knowledge imparted in this book, coupled with practice, you will be able to work on building your own websites or coding your own projects.

In your further study, I recommend that you learn and take on advanced topics such as troubleshooting in JavaScript, explore different frameworks and libraries, and expand your knowledge in using regular expressions.

I would also strongly recommend that you learn other programming languages, so that you may be able to take your knowledge to the next level, and become a top-class programmer. Because you have gone through this course, you will be astonished to find that learning other languages is easier than expected, for JavaScript has strikingly paved the way for you. I recommend Python or Java as the best languages to learn next.